How Deep Is Deep Ecology?

with an essay-review on Woman's Freedom

by George Bradford

 Times Change PRESS

Printed at Common Wealth Printing Co., Hadley, Massachusetts, U.S.A.

First printing

Times Change Press
Editorial office: Box 1380, Ojai, California 93023
Sales office: c/o Publishers Services, Box 2510, Novato, California 94948

This book's principal essays first appeared in slightly different form in *Fifth Estate* newspaper, P. O. Box 02548, Detroit, Michigan 48202.

Typesetting, layout, and design work donated by Freddie Baer, with kind assistance from daniel g

Cover graphic by Cornelis Massys, *The Blind Leading the Blind*

Library of Congress Cataloging-in-Publication Data

Bradford, George, 1952-
    How deep is deep ecology?

    Bibliography: p.
      1. Human ecology—Philosophy. 2. Population.
3. Earth First! (Organization) 4. Women's rights.
5. Birth control. I. Title.
GF21.B64 1989   304.2   89-4640
ISBN 0-87810-035-0

Table of Contents

Foreword

I first came across the *Fifth Estate* containing "How Deep is Deep Ecology?" in an anarchist bookstore on a visit to Sydney, Australia. I knew very little of deep ecology, but I had attended some Earth First! meetings, had bought the newspaper, and had been mostly inspired but occasionally upset by what I'd heard and read.

Bradford's essay placed these mixed reactions in perspective and gave me enough insight into deep ecology to see that both the positive and negative aspects of Earth First! might be attributable to a philosophical point of view rather than being merely expressions of individual personalities. I thought it was a valuable critique of a philosophy and a movement that are in many ways perceptive and admirable and which have thus captured the imagination and loyalty of many energetic and caring human beings. It is this very success that renders any serious shortcomings of philosophy so distressful and even dangerous, in a world that is in desperate need of such insights as deep ecology has fostered and of the kind of brave examples many of its people have set.

It was obvious to me that Bradford was writing from just such concern, and that the essay had in some ways been a painful undertaking for him. I thought that he had succeeded in making clear his sharing of perspective with much that deep ecology is supposed to be about, and that many who use the deep-ecology label could read it profitably without any feeling of being put down.

As the new editor of Times Change Press, I had been eager to resume its publication of new titles. I soon decided that these essays afforded a fine opportunity to bring to a larger audience something I found important. This is the first new title our press has brought out since 1977.

Bradford, who continues to write on the theme of radical ecology for the *Fifth Estate*, felt that the essay-review on "Woman's Freedom: Key to the Population Question" should be included as well, since it addresses an aspect of the population problem that tends to be slighted by deep ecologists and others who express grave concern about overpopulation.

The *Fifth Estate* is addressed to activists, and that means that it has a somewhat special vocabulary and tends toward sternness in its critiques. The *Fifth Estate* group argued that some of its special words should be retained, as they merit wider use, relating, as they do, to significant phenomena and attitudes that cannot be succinctly expressed without them.

I hope that the sometimes forceful opinions will be seen in context, and not as an attack on what is worthwhile in deep ecology. I have, for example, a little knowledge of public positions taken by Arne Naess, who may have coined the phrase "deep ecology." In my opinion, these positions clearly demonstrate that he — and, by extension, other less-well-known deep ecologists — have little sympathy for misanthropy or racism. By the time this sees print Naess's own book, *Ecology, Community and Lifestyle: Outline of an Ecosophy* (Cambridge University Press), will finally be in print in English, and readers can judge his writings for themselves.

True defenders of Mother Earth will see easily enough that Bradford is on their side. He and his comrades' purpose, clearly, is to encourage human endeavor toward creating a society that will enrich and extend humankind's stay on this planet, amidst the countless wonders of nature and the vital creativity of our fellows.

— *Lamar Hoover*
Times Change Press

Preface

Describing a "planetary dimension" of contemporary culture that linked the desire for an authentic life to the health of the natural world itself, Theodore Roszak wrote in his inspired book *Person/Planet* of his certainty that "within the next generation, there will emerge a well-developed body of ecological theory that illuminates this subtle interrelation and gives it enough political force to displace the inherited ideologies of industrial society." That was in 1978. Though we did not come to read his prediction until much later, the expansion and dissemination of just such theory has been the project of the radical antiauthoritarian journal *Fifth Estate*, in which the following essays appeared, since about the same time that Roszak's book was published. These particular essays on deep ecology and the population question, which appeared in late 1987 and early 1988, were in fact an attempt to bring radical social critique to bear on the growing, yet amorphous, ecological conscience.

Now that George Bush has declared himself an environmentalist and *Time* magazine has named this plundered Earth "planet of the year," now that everyone expresses ecological concern, from the people living in contaminated communities to the businesses that contaminate them, it is time to regard environmentalism as a movement whose real promise remains unfulfilled. The insights of ecology have been debased to everyday clichés while the actual plunder and poisoning are accelerating. The environmental movement itself has to a great degree been integrated as a kind of corrective mechanism into the operational logic of the industrial-capitalist machine presently strip-mining the biosphere. This is because the environmentalists have focused not on the root-causes of ecological destruction but on the symptoms. Thus the radical critique which informs these essays is very appropriate, since *radical* means going to the root.

But it should be emphasized that the essays were not academic evaluations. Their purpose was rather to begin a dialogue with those people in the more intransigent, "no-compromise," direct-action wing of the environmental movement who might share our vision. They were a challenge from one group of activists to another to debate and discuss perspectives and goals. Ultimately, the challenge was taken up, and we made many positive connections through the ensuing discussions. Many themes only touched on here were explored further in subsequent issues of *Fifth Estate* and elsewhere. The reader may write us at P. O. Box 02548, Detroit, Michigan 48202 to inquire about further work on these matters.

These essays do not presume to discuss every aspect or every representative of deep ecology. Nor do they attempt to judge the entire green/ecology phenomenon, but they are nevertheless relevant to its fundamental concerns. Because they examine the tension between causes and symptoms, between civilization's power complex and the resulting ecological degradation, between oppositional movements and their reabsorption by the system they oppose, between ideology and theory, they will prove valuable to that discourse anticipated by Roszak and to the worldwide movement that will make use of it to advance a visionary social revolution.

I use the first-person plural here to describe the production of these essays because *Fifth Estate* has always been a collective theoretical and practical project, with particular authorship only a function of circumstances or individual mania. I want to thank and acknowledge my comrades at the *FE* for reading and editing, and for the entire spectrum of activities that have made it possible. I extend these thanks as well to Freddie Baer and daniel g, of San Francisco, who collaborated with us in editing, layout, and graphics.

Lamar Hoover of Times Change Press has contributed greatly to streamlining, clarifying, and improving the text for this book edition. He has warned me that readers may have difficulties with some of the somewhat idiosyncratic language of the radical political discourse in which we participate. I can only hope that most of the terms are relatively self-explanatory, and have insisted on maintaining those that I think could not be replaced by more common words without altering their meaning. The modern world is a totalitarian affair in which words occasionally have been reconstituted, stolen, or alchemized to describe complex phenomena. My use of words reflects not only my influences but also my desires. In linguistics, as in social matters, anarchist creativity and risk-taking are the best approach.

— *George Bradford*

How Deep Is Deep Ecology?
A Challenge to
Radical Environmentalism

"In every perception of nature there is actually present the whole of society." — *Theodor Adorno,* Aesthetic Theory

"The human race could go extinct, and I, for one, would not shed any tears." — *Dave Foreman of Earth First!, a deep-ecology environmental organization*

Books and publications reviewed in this essay:

Overshoot: The Ecological Basis of Revolutionary Change, by William R. Catton, Jr., University of Illinois Press, Urbana, 1980.

Deep Ecology: Living As If Nature Mattered, by Bill Devall and George Sessions, Gibbs M. Smith, Inc./Peregrine Smith Books, Salt Lake City, 1985.

Deep Ecology, edited by Michael Tobias, Avant Books, San Diego, 1985.

Food First: Beyond the Myth of Scarcity, revised and updated, by Frances Moore Lappé and Joseph Collins, Ballantine Books, New York, 1978; Institute for Food and Development Policy, 145 Ninth Street, San Francisco, California 94103.

Inside the Third World, by Paul Harrison, Penguin Books, New York, 1981.

Earth First!, published eight times a year by the Earth First! movement, from P.O. Box 2358, Lewiston, ME 04241.

Ecology and the Necessity for Social Critique

The present ruination of the earth in the wake of widening industrial plagues is a situation which appears to have no meaningful or comparable precedent. Mass extinctions of species, industrial contamination, runaway development, war, starvation, and megatechnic catastrophes have led to a sense of deep disquiet and mounting terror about the fate of the planet and of all life. There is also a growing recognition that the environmental crisis is the crisis of a civilization destructive in its essence to nature and humanity.

"All thinking worthy of the name," writes Lewis Mumford in *The Myth of the Machine*, "must become ecological." Indeed, ecology, the word that sees nature as a household, has become a household word. Envisioning the world as an interlocking, organic whole, ecology attempts to transcend mechanistic, fragmentary, and instrumental perspectives. But ecology as a scientific discipline is itself fragmentary; the notion of nature as a system can be as mechanistic and instrumental as previous scientific modes employed by industrial civilization, as the contemporary convergence of cybernetics, systems theory, and biotechnology attests.

Ecology as science speculates, often with profound insight, about nature's movement and the impact of human activities on it. But it is ambiguous, or silent, about the social context that generates those activities and how it might change. In and of itself, ecology offers no social critique, so where critique flows directly from ecological discourse, subsuming the complexities of the social into a picture of undifferentiated humanity as a species, it goes astray and is frequently vapid. Often it is employed only to justify different political ideologies, masking social conflicts in pseudoscientific generalizations. Social Darwinism, with its Malthusian legitimation of capital accumulation and human immiseration during the nineteenth century, is a trenchant example of the ideological utilization of scientific discourse — an example which unfortunately remains, like all fragmentary ideologies in the modern world, to plague us today.

Whether or not an entirely coherent nature philosophy is even possible, the nagging question of humanity's relation to the natural world and its parallel significance to our relations among ourselves has become a major issue (and the most important one) in the last few years. A deepening revulsion against the industrial-work culture and the shock at the obliteration of ecosystems, species, cultures, and peoples have inspired an emerging anti-industrial counterculture and a rediscovery of the lifeways of our primal roots. This has led to some degree to a convergence of environmental and antiwar movements; with it has come a significant radicalization and developing strategy of mass direct action and sabotage against megatechnic projects and the war machine. Anarchism, too, and antiauthoritarian ideas in general, have had no small influence on this movement. Deepening critiques of industrial-capitalist civilization (in its private Western form, and its bureaucratic Eastern form, both of them statist), technology, science, and the mystique of progress have contributed to a new, if diverse, philosophical orientation.

Among ecological thinkers there has been an attempt to move beyond the limitations of ecological science toward a nature philosophy and earth-based culture. Some have proposed a new perspective, deep ecology, as an emerging social model or "new paradigm" for humanity's relationship with nature. Deep ecology is a rather eclectic mixture of writings and influences, drawing on the one hand from romantic and transcendentalist writings, nature poetry, Eastern mysticism, and the land wisdom of primal peoples, and on the other hand from general ecological science, including modern Malthusianism. This far-from-coherent mixture is not entirely separate from ecology in general. At the same time, an organized deep-ecology action movement has appeared, with a newspaper and many local chapters and contacts, as well as its own mythos, history, intellectual luminaries, and militant chieftains.

This group, Earth First!, was founded in the early 1980s as a radical alternative to the mainstream environmental organizations, "a true Earth-radical group" that saw wilderness preservation as its keystone. "In *any* decision, consideration for the health of the Earth must come first," wrote a founder, Dave Foreman, in the October 1981 *Progressive* magazine. Wilderness preservation means not only to protect remaining wilderness but to "withdraw huge areas as inviolate natural sanctuaries from the depredations of modern industry and technology."

Earth First! claims to be nonhierarchic, nonbureaucratic, and decentralized; many of its adherents consider themselves anarchists. It practices and encourages an explicitly Luddite form of direct action against the machinery of developers, and favors tree-spiking and other tactics to stop deforestation by lumber corporations—all these described as "monkeywrenching," after Edward Abbey's novel about eco-saboteurs, *The Monkeywrench Gang*. Its people have done much to oppose development projects and protect national parks, using demonstrations, guerrilla theatre, and civil disobedience. Their newspaper is also an excellent source for information on rainforest destruction, battles over wilderness and old-growth forests, defense of habitat for bears and others species — in short, for environmental confrontations all over the world. They have definitely played a positive and creative role in encouraging and publicizing a more intransigent environmentalism that is willing to go beyond letter-writing and lobbying. In *Earth First!* there is little information on struggles against toxic wastes or megatechnic development in the cities, or of antimilitarist struggles. Starting from what they call deep-ecological principles, they see their efforts at wilderness preservation as central.

Does deep ecology represent an emergent paradigm for an earth-based culture? Is it the coherent culmination of the anti-industrial tradition?

"Biocentrism" Versus "Anthropocentrism"

Deep ecology as a perspective was originated by Norwegian writer Arne Naess in the 1970s and remains an eclectic and ambiguous current. To date, the two most influential books in English dealing explicitly with the subject are anthologies containing a mixture of writings, sometimes complementary, sometimes contradictory. *Deep Ecology* (Avant Books, 1984), edited by Michael Tobias, is a collection of poetry and essays from writers like William Catton, George Sessions, Murray Bookchin, and Garrett Hardin. The essayists are widely divergent, the poetry a mix of general nature and ecological themes. Another collection, *Deep Ecology: Living As If Nature Mattered* (Peregrine Smith Books, 1985), is written and edited by George Sessions and Bill Devall and is probably the more complete book, made up of essays by the editors and quotes from a myriad of sources. The Tobias volume, nevertheless, has several useful essays for understanding the perspective (including a long philosophical essay by Bookchin anticipating some of the problems in it).

It was Arne Naess who in 1973 described deep ecology as an attempt "to ask deeper questions." This "ecosophy," as he called it, consciously shifted "from science to wisdom" by addressing humanity's relationship with nature, since "ecology as a science does not ask what kind of society would be best for maintaining a particular ecosystem." Sessions sees it as a "new philosophy of nature," and one text from a green network, quoted in his anthology, describes such ecological consciousness as "a proper understanding of the purposes and workings of nature" that does not "impose an ideology on it."

The philosophy has as its basic premises the interrelatedness of all life, a biotic equality for all organisms (including those for which human beings have no "use" or which might even be harmful to us), and a rejection of "anthropocentrism" (the belief that human beings are separate from, superior to, and more important than the rest of nature). Anthropocentrism, they feel, underlies human arrogance toward and exploitation of the natural world. They call for a new "land ethic," after environmentalist writer Aldo Leopold, not only to restore a harmonious balance in nature, but to answer a fundamental human need to experience untrammeled wilderness and to live in harmony with the planet. Many of these concerns are not unique to deep ecology; at the *Fifth Estate* newspaper, for example, we have made such a reconciliation with the natural world a central focus for the last decade.

The appeal of a biocentric orientation and its critique of the conquest of nature that has characterized all state civilizations (particularly Western civilization and capitalism) is undeniable. Seeing human beings as members of a biotic community may at least suggest the question of "what kind of society would be best" for living in harmony with the earth. This, of course, is the vision of primal peoples, the animist mutualism and rootedness that is in everyone's past. As Luther Standing Bear said of his people in his book *Land of the Spotted Eagle*, "The Lakota was a true naturist — a lover of Nature." His people "loved the earth, the attachment growing with age. . . . Kinship with all creatures of the earth, sky, and water was a real and active principle . . . and so close did some of the Lakota come to their feathered and furred friends that in true brotherhood they spoke a common tongue."

The rejection of "human chauvinism," as deep ecologist John Seed puts it in his essay, "Anthropocentrism" (in the Devall/Sessions anthology), is a rediscovery of this view. "'I am protecting the rainforest,'" Seed writes, "develops to 'I am part of the rainforest protecting myself. I am that part of the rainforest recently emerged into thinking.'"

The wisdom of this vision is clear; the present apocalypse that we are experiencing is the culmination of the hubris which wants to bring all of nature under human control, either through rapacious devastation or "benign" meddling. When one considers how people live in this high-energy-consumption society, with its hatred and contempt for life and nature, with its demonic development projects that gouge the earth and destroy myriad life forms to create the empty, alienated civilization of computerized nihilism, even the response of misanthropy is understandable — such as naturalist John Muir's comment that "if a war of races should occur between the wild beast and Lord Man, I would be tempted to sympathize with the bears. . . ." Deep ecology claims that that time has come.

As poetic commentary, Muir's misanthropy is commendable. But it must be remembered that human beings are animals too, and the same forces that are destroying the bears have destroyed many human beings and cultures, and are undermining all human life as well. The rejection of biotic hierarchy, and of "man" as the pinnacle and lord of creation (the model for all hierarchies), is crucial to a reconciliation with the natural world, but the deep-ecology critique of anthropocentrism is itself mired in ideology.

In opposition to "humanism" (defined rather simplistically as the ideology of human superiority and the legitimacy to exploit nature for human purposes), deep ecology claims to be a perspective taken from outside human discourse and politics, from the point of view of nature as a whole. Of course, it is a problematic claim, to say the least, since deep ecologists have developed a viewpoint based on human, socially generated, and historically evolved insights into nature, in order to design an orientation toward human society. At any rate, any vision of nature and humanity's place in it that is the production of human discourse is by definition going to be to some degree "anthropocentric," imposing as it does a human, symbolic discourse on the nonhuman.

Deep ecologists reject other forms of environmentalism, such as technocratic resource conservation, as anthropocentric because they are framed in terms of utility to human beings. And, criticizing animal liberation, Sessions and Devall argue that it simply extends moral and political categories of legal rights from the human world to nature, thus furthering the human conquest of nature.

But deep ecology's "intuition. . . that all things in this biosphere have an equal right to live and blossom" is the same projection of human social-political categories onto nature — a legalistic and bourgeois-humanist anthropocentrism itself. Ecology confirms the animist vision of interrelatedness, but when expressed in the ideological terms of this society, it denatures and colonizes animism, reducing it to a kind of economics or juridical, legal formalism. Neither animals nor primal peoples recognized or conferred abstract legal rights, but lived in harmony and mutualism, including a mutualism of predation of other species to fulfill their needs and desires. Human subsistence was bound up with natural cycles and not in opposition to them; people did not envision an alienated "humanity versus nature" dualism (which, whether one takes "nature's side" or "humanity's," is an ideology of this civilization), but rather "humanized" nature by interacting mythically and symbolically with it.

When ecological "antihumanism" (justly) rejects technocratic resource management, it does so for the wrong reasons. The dualism of its formulation takes the technocratic reduction of nature to resources for an undifferentiated species activity based on supposed biological need. While human beings and institutions that actively engage in the destruction of nature must be stopped by any means necessary and as soon as possible, it should not automatically be assumed that they are acting out the biological destiny of the species; that would be to take at face value the corporate and state rationalizations for exploitation ("we do it all for you"). The human social context that produces this aberrant destructiveness is not readily explained by ecological analysis.

Deep ecologists err when they see the pathological operationalism of industrial civilization as a species-generated problem rather than as one generated by social phenomena that must be studied in their own right. Concealing socially generated conflicts behind an ideology of "natural law," they contradictorily insist on and deny a unique position for human beings while neglecting the centrality of the social in environmental devastation. Consequently, they have no really "deep" critique of the state, empire, technology, or capital, reducing the complex web of human relations to a simplistic, abstract, scientistic caricature.

Thus humanity as a species, or a voracious human self-interest acting through "humanism," is blamed for ecological degradation by most (if not necessarily all) deep ecologists, particularly the American adherents close to Earth First!. This formulation, shared by many people in the U.S. conservation movement, tends to overlook the fact that preservation of wilderness and defense of natural integrity and diversity is essential to human survival also. There is no isolated "intrinsic worth" but an interrelated dependency that includes us all.

The Problem of Human Intervention

Another confusion in the critique of anthropocentrism is the rejection of human stewardship of nature. The notion of intervention is anthropocentric to these deep ecologists; they associate it with genetic manipulation, scientific forestry management, and resource development (actually extraction) for "human needs." But they offer only an alternative form of management. As Sessions and Devall write, "Our first principle is to encourage agencies, legislators, property owners and managers to consider flowing with rather than forcing natural resources." They call for "interim management" and technological intervention. This ambiguity (and ingenuousness about agencies, legislators, and the rest) informs this entire discussion. Their description of policy decisions "based on sound ecological principles" sounds like a picture of *present* agencies and their self-justifications. The detailed wilderness proposals in *Earth First!* are also an example of a notion of human stewardship.

And despite their lack of sympathy for mass technics, they have no critique of technology as a system or of its relation to capitalist institutions. In this same anthology, we read that while humans "have no right to reduce richness and diversity except to satisfy *vital* needs" (a rather ambiguous qualification), snowmobiles are deemed "necessary today to satisfy vital needs" of northern peoples such as the Innuit. So, in with the snowmobiles must slip the industrial apparatus and petroleum-based energy economy that are necessary to produce

11

and use them. In fact, they argue, culture itself "requires advanced technology," so we end up with a somehow "greened" version of the present world, with industrialism and a technicized culture intact — presumably with those quaint native dances on television to preserve "diversity."

Capitalist institutions are barely looked at as the major perpetrators of environmental devastation they are, even though these authors do recognize "the possible destruction of up to twenty-five percent of all species on Earth due to 'business-as-usual' economic growth and development during the next forty to sixty years." Speaking of the unintended consequences of technology, they refer to the agricultural crisis in California's Central Valley, where the agribusiness "which claims as its goal, 'feeding the hungry of the world,' is now creating an unhealthy, almost unfit environment for many human inhabitants of the Valley." Here they seem to take corporate propaganda at face value, so that technological short-sightedness and the "humanist" goal of "feeding the world" become the cause of the problem, rather than capitalist looting, which degrades the natural integrity of the valley not to feed people but to line the investors' pockets.

These deep ecologists claim to ask deeper questions, but they do not recognize that this might require deeper analysis of human society. So the "nonideological" perspective ends up taking politics in a capitalist democracy for granted, recommending a rather confused kind of "direct action in politics or lobbying" (Sessions and Devall). For these deep-ecology theorists, direct action is reduced to lobbying, and presumably to electoral politics (how many trees got chopped down when Jerry Brown was governor of California and the environmentalists cozied up to him?). Nowhere is this "working-within-the-system" centrism questioned; it is simply assumed. We also get a fetish of nonviolence from Sessions and Devall, and a reformism that centers on seeking wilderness proposals and that wishes to "secure" nature "against degradation caused by warfare and other hostile acts." Their naiveté about securing nature against war is equalled by their simplistic view of international politics and the global economy, particularly the relations between industrial nations and the Third World.

The deep-ecology perspective insists that everything is interrelated and sees this recognition as "subversive to an exploitive attitude and culture" (Sessions, in the Tobias anthology). But ecological reductionism fails to see the interrelatedness of the global corporate-capitalist system and empire on the one hand, and environmental catastrophe on the other. This is far from subversive — despite the courageous and imaginative acts of many militants who act against the tentacles of the planetary machine in the name of deep ecology. In fact, the absence of a critique of capital is a real impediment to the generalization of authentic resistance to the exploitive-extractive empire which is presently devouring the earth, because it mystifies the power relations of this society and squanders the possibility for linking the human victims of the machine in different sectors. Anthropocentrism or not, humans are the only beings in a position to wage effective war against the empires and articulate an earth-based culture and a renewal of the land. [1]

"Malthus Was Right"

While deep ecologists may consider their perspective a "new paradigm," its Malthusian component is a commonplace of current ideology. In fact, "too many people" is one of the automatic responses made to any criticism of industrialism and the state: present numbers, we are always assured by ecologist, corporate developer, Marxist and capitalist alike, could never be supported in a nonindustrial, sustainable society.

Most deep ecologists accept Malthus' proposition — that human population exponentially outstrips food production — as an essential support for their orientation (though it is certainly arguable that deep-ecological thinking need not be Malthusian). The slogan "Malthus Was Right" is even peddled as a bumpersticker by Earth First!. William J. Catton, Jr., who is quoted and published in both anthologies, is a leading modernizer of Malthus, and his book *Overshoot: The Ecological Basis for Revolutionary Change* (University of Illinois Press, 1980) has become a bible of sorts to the deep ecologists (even those, one would surmise, who haven't read it).

Population growth is certainly a cause for concern, perhaps even alarm. More than 900 million people are presently malnourished or starving, and hunger spreads with the rising numbers. But Malthusian empiricism sees many hungry mouths and concludes that there are too many people and not enough resources to keep them alive. Scarcity and famine are thus explained as natural phenomena, inevitable, irrevocable, even benign. The pseudo-objectivity of scientific ideology is probably nowhere more profoundly expressed than in this Malthusian model. If, astonishingly, it is still necessary to argue against Malthus a century and a half later, it is because people know so little history.

Malthusian ideology emerged from the crucible of early industrialism and the immiseration and class conflict that came in its wake. As people were driven from their lands and craft workers were dispossessed by industry, masses of displaced people were shovelled into mills and mines, ground up to accumulate profit, and replaced by the hungry unemployed who followed them. As the English commons (where rural people might grow their own food) were seized by wealthy landowners and sheep farmers, even the food and help to which they had traditionally been entitled during hard times in feudal society came under attack.

Malthus was only the most celebrated of the many pseudo-philosophers who sanctioned class brutality by applying the economics of Adam Smith and its notion of a "natural" and self-regulating political economy to "natural law." With the advent of classical economics, the previously held notion of a "just wage" had disappeared; now the obligation to help the poor went with it. The surplus of workers that was so good for business and kept wages down came to be seen as a surplus in population. From his pulpit and in his essays, the good parson Thomas Malthus argued that people's animal power of multiplication would eventually run up against the constricting walls of scarcity, and concluded that feeding people who might otherwise starve would only lead them to procreate and increase generalized misery.

Against the rising revolutionary tide in France and the writings of utopian disciples of Rousseau, who attributed vice and misery to the corruption of human institutions and civilization, he posed "deeper seated causes of impurity," namely his "principle of population." In answer to the anarchist utopian William Godwin, who argued after Rousseau that in a society where people lived "in the midst of plenty and where all shared alike the bounties of nature," misery, oppression, servility, and other vices would disappear, Malthus solemnly declared: "Man cannot live in the midst of plenty. All cannot share alike the bounties of nature." Contrary to the vision of humanity's natural state as one of "ease, happiness, and comparative leisure," he argued, in the dour vein of Thomas Hobbes's vision of a state of war of all against all, that population was *always and everywhere* pressing against available food supply. So if subsistence should improve, population would rise with it, and pressure on the food supply would begin anew.` For the sake of civilization and human progress, there was no alternative. "Man as he really is," he pronounced, "is inert, sluggish, and averse from labor, unless compelled by necessity." Therefore, instead of aiding the poor, "we should . . . court the return of the plague."

Malthus's numerical formula, which he worked out assiduously in his book, elaborately contrasting the abstract differential between geometric and arithmetical growth, was the most compelling part of his proposition. But his argument was essentially circular and reflected in Newtonian fashion only a tendency or *capacity* for exponential population growth in a hypothetical situation in which no checks on population were present. Too many imponderable factors were involved in his calculations, and as Gertrude Himmelfarb wryly observed in her introduction to the 1960 edition of *On Population*, "The difficulties, as Malthus might have said, increased geometrically." [2]

If, as Jeremy Rifkin argues in his important, though flawed, book *Algeny*, "there is no neutral naturalism," it is clear that the acceptance of Malthus's proposition had little to do with its actual merits. Within its own terms and framework it was irrefutable, but Malthus's schema was as anthropocentric as it was ideological. Outside its social context, it would have remained merely speculation. As it was, it legitimated brutal oppression and dispossession of entire classes of people. As Himmelfarb remarks, its logic "was the logic of Adam Smith and there was nothing in the principle of population that was not implied in the now 'classical' principles of political economy. . . . Malthus only made more dramatic what Smith had earlier had insisted upon: that men were as much subject to the laws of supply and demand as were commodities. . . ."

A Struggle for Survival

Darwin's theoretical formulations came from the same social context. And if Malthus's proposition appealed to Darwin for its suggestion of natural selection through a "struggle for life" (a term that Malthus himself had used), it appealed to the English ruling classes for the same reason. Darwin's theory, despite a wealth of keen observation, was, in Rifkin's words, "a reflection of the industrial state of mind" that anthropocentrized nature by imposing economic categories on it. As Mumford writes, "Darwin was in fact imputing to nature the ugly characteristics of Victorian capitalism and colonialism. So far from offsetting the effects of the mechanical world picture, this doctrine only unhappily offered a touch of cold-blooded brutality. . . ."

The struggle for survival (a parallel of the human struggle) was the motor force of progress and evolution. "All organic beings," Darwin argued in *The Origin of Species*, were "striving to seize upon each place in the economy of nature." Yield, output, and the motive of efficiency inform all his work. "Hard cash paid down over and over again" was the "test of inherited superiority." In an argument derivative of Adam Smith's notion of economic progress, even the evolution of simple to more complex organisms represented a kind of physiological division of labor. And European colonialism was legitimated too, as it justified, in Darwin's words, the "extermination of 'less intellectual lower races' by the more intelligent higher races." There was "one general law," he argued, "leading to the advancement of all organic beings, namely, multiply, vary, let the strongest live and the weakest die."

It would be careless and inaccurate to argue that Darwin's insights were entirely the product of bourgeois mystification and scientism. There was even the implicit insight in Malthus that infinite technological progress and population growth would ultimately crash against natural finite limits — a point overlooked by the utopians and their bourgeois, Marxist and syndicalist descendants. But if in Darwin, particularly, there was an ambiguity between the organic understanding he developed and the mechanistic, economistic terms in which it was often expressed, there was no such ambiguity in the Darwinism, and its offspring, the Social Darwinism, that followed.

Social Darwinism and Malthusianism became enshrined in modern ideology, in the viewpoints of the powerful classes and the powerful nations. As Darwin's contemporary Herbert Spencer put it, humanity's very well-being depended on this struggle for survival: "The poverty of the incapable, the distresses that come upon the imprudent, the starvation of the idle, and those shoulderings aside of the weak by the strong, which leave so many 'in shallows and in miseries,' are the decrees of a large, far-seeing benevolence." By way of this "conjurer's trick," as Engels called their formulations (though he too suffered from its determinist, productivist methodology), bourgeois economic doctrine was transferred to nature, and then back again to human society and history to prove its validity as eternal natural law. [3]

Modernizing Malthusianism

So the deep-ecology position on overpopulation, rather than being part of a "new paradigm," is part of an old one, the economistic Malthusian theory. It has also been pretty standard fare in ecological writings since Darwin. [4] Nevertheless, the overpopulation thesis is still compelling, especially when one looks at a graph of human population growth since prehistory, with the right-hand side shooting up precipitously in the last two or three centuries. The population question, as neo-Malthusian ecologist Paul Ehrlich (author of *The Population Bomb*) remarks, is "a numbers game," but imagine a country like Bangladesh, with its large population and all the problems of private land tenure, peonage, and institutional scarcity that it faces, doubling in size in the span of a generation. As human numbers climb to six, seven, eight billion in the new few decades, it is fair to ask what possibility there will be for liberatory societies living in harmony with the natural world. And techno-fix responses — from fusion power to super-bioengineered agriculture to space colonies — are either absurd fantasies or "solutions" that are worse than the problem itself.

At some point in population growth, neither natural integrity nor human freedom is possible. But despite Malthusian numerology, that point is not self-evident. Consequently, overpopulation may be one source of the present world hunger crisis, but it takes a leap of faith to conclude automatically that famine is purely the result of "natural laws" when it occurs in a class society with a market economy and private ownership of land. Ecology reduced to ideology tends to simplify what is complex when its analysis ignores the interrelations within human society. But the interpretation of hunger is deadly serious because on it depends how ecologists, and all of us, respond to a whole complex of associated problems. Ideas have material consequences, so it is the responsibility of deep ecologists to examine their premises carefully. These premises find their most thorough expression in William Catton's book, *Overshoot*.

While Catton's book does not start from an explicitly deep-ecological perspective, the Malthusian premises it shares with deep ecology and the way it has been employed in both deep-ecology anthologies make it an important text for this discussion. Based on the ecological concept of "carrying capacity" (the capacity of an ecosystem to support a given population of a species in a sustainable and renewable manner), Catton's thesis is that "human population has long ago moved into a dangerous phase of the 'boom-bust' cycle of population growth and decline." He explains in the Tobias anthology, "Carrying capacity, though variable and not easily or always measurable, must be taken into account to understand the human predicament."

Of course Catton does far more than take this ecological concern into account. He creates a theory of history around it, attributing the rise of state civilizations, technological development, war and imperial rivalry, economic crisis and unemployment, political ideology and cultural mores, revolt and revolution all to population pressures. It is an ambitious theory, but it follows the same economistic logic and mathematical mystification as that of Malthus. Catton's book reveals how scientism, the lack of a social critique, and captivity to a paradigm or model can lead to misinterpretation.

Catton's view starts from a Darwinian perspective of a competitive struggle for survival between species. Human beings have historically followed a process of "takeover" of carrying capacity ("diverting" resources from other species to themselves), "essentially at the expense of [the earth's] other inhabitants." But human expansion inevitably had to come up against the limits of scarcity, of the land's carrying capacity. Only the discovery of new territories and new forms of extraction would forestall population crash. The first leap was the "horticultural revolution," which made it possible for "a minuscule but increasing fraction of any human tribe to devote its time to activities other than obtaining sustenance." With this increased human "management" of the biosphere, carrying capacity was increased, and with it, human population.

The next significant stage in development occurs at the end of the European Middle Ages (and this book has a very Euramerican focus), when the known world was "saturated with population," making life intolerable and threatening a population crash. The discovery of the Americas, however, changed everything. "This sudden and impressive surplus of carrying capacity" shattered the medieval vision of changelessness, and laid the foundations for an "Age of Exuberance," with its "cornucopian paradigm." "In a habitat that now seemed limitless, life would be lived abundantly." New beliefs and new human relationships were born from the increased carrying capacity, including a revolution in invention and technology (though elsewhere he argues that the development of technology is a result of population pressure rather than of this "exuberance") and a democratic world view.

But as population quickly expanded, the next stage of expansion of carrying capacity was the development of "phantom carrying capacity," extracting only temporarily available, nonrenewable resources to support burgeoning numbers, a "drawdown" form of takeover which relies on petroleum, minerals, etc. This dependence led to "overshoot" and the present "post-exuberant age," in which human numbers have long exceeded the long-term, renewable carrying capacity of the environment, bringing about inevitable "crash" or "die-off" of the population. "There are already more human beings alive than the world's renewable resources can perpetually support," he argues. Carrying capacity is also being diminished by toxic industrialism, "unavoidably created by our life processes."

While there are many possible responses to this crisis, including revolutionary upheaval or faith in technology, he asserts that only an ecological paradigm, which recognizes carrying capacity limits and the need to reduce human numbers, will work. "The cumulative potential of the human species," he writes, repeating Malthus, "exceeds the carrying capacity of its habitat." Having stated this incorporeal truism regarding a *potentiality*, he concludes, "No interpretation of recent history can be valid unless it takes these two factors and this relation between them into account."

Catton's book is not without its insights and thoughtful observations, and his arguments are often persuasive, relying as they do on the obvious — the destruction of nature by civilization, the increase of human numbers, the finite limits of the earth. Unfortunately, his thesis is only a rehash of Malthus: scientifically reductionist, simplistic, and highly ideological. Attempting to turn "ecological principles into sociological principles," he turns sociological distortions into natural law.

Scientific Reductionism

There is a kind of inverted anthropocentrism suggested in Catton's idea of takeover and interspecies competition for resources that, one suspects, secretly wishes to eliminate humans altogether from nature in order to impose some hypothetical balance (a view held without irony by some deep ecologists). This is the struggle for survival and law of the jungle left over from Social Darwinism. But it is also possible to postulate a mutualist equilibrium between humans and the rest of nature throughout the vast majority of our sojourn on this planet, in which human subsistence has even nurtured and encouraged the life of other species. [5] Catton's paleontology is also skewed, with its implicit Hobbesian picture of primitive life as a miserable struggle for subsistence and its facile description of the origins of agriculture and the emergence of hierarchies. His historical theory of stages is patterned after the standard textbook model of progress.

The real shortcomings of Catton's thesis are most apparent in his historiography and analysis of the modern epoch. His scientific reductionism misinterprets the rise of capitalism and present capitalist society. His simplification of the whole convergence of cultural-historic developments — rising mercantilism and industrialism, the spread of invention, statification and national consolidation, exploration and conquest, the slave trade, and more — to a species "exuberance" (like bacteria in a petri dish) due to increased carrying capacity, is biological determinism at its crudest. He paints a rosy picture of Europe as it was depopulated in the mass flight to the Americas, overlooking the fact that despite "increased carrying capacity" there, conditions in Europe *worsened* for most people during the conquest.

That the riches in America and the cheap labor of her indigenous and imported slaves provided raw material and "increased carrying capacity" for emergent capitalism goes without saying. But there is little or nothing in Catton's history about this "original accumulation" that paid for industrialization, which is why he fails as well to understand the character of U.S. civilization. The "abundance and liberty," he writes, had "ecological prerequisites" — though he doesn't explain what were the prerequisites of the slavocratic, exterminist, repressive side of the civilization. (Nor does his model illuminate the contrast between North America and Latin America, which had the same "ecological prerequisites," yet an exceedingly different social character, leading to that oppressive and uneven relationship between them with which we should all be thoroughly familiar.)

Catton's portrayal of U.S. development is an oddly formulated apology for empire. Extolling the frontier, he attributes American democracy to a simple surplus carrying capacity (an argument, coincidentally, which implies that current scarcity must inevitably lead to authoritarian rule). "A carrying capacity surplus facilitates development and maintenance of democratic institutions," he declares, while "a carrying capacity deficit weakens and undermines them." Thus political differences between the U.S. and Europe were ecological: "Europe was full of people; America was full of potential." Such sloppiness not only effaces English and French (revolutionary) democracy and other libertarian forms from the picture, it overlooks a country like Russia, also relatively empty of people and "full of potential," which suffered under despotism and autocracy.

This pseudohistory is mixed with sociological-ecological clichés, and ends in patriotic fervor. Low population density, he tells us, renders "human equality . . . feasible, even probable." (Saudi Arabia?) U.S. history, therefore, "has thus exemplified the dependence of political liberty upon ecological foundations." He makes no reference here to slavery, the conquest of northern Mexico, the extermination of the Indians, the interventions into Central America, the bitter class conflicts in mines and mills. And he leaves us with a high-school textbook picture of the country: "Settlers in the New World *did* create a new and inspired form of government in a land of opportunity. . . . Americans *did* win the west. . . . A great nation was built in the wilderness. . . ."

Our Yankee Doodle Dandy concludes in an outburst of political cant we've heard from Daniel Boone to Ronald Reagan: America "tried honestly and generously to share the fruits of its frontier experience with people in other societies overseas. . . . " (like Vietnam and Nicaragua!). But as the empire extended its domination overseas, this sharing came to nothing, since "American imperialism was essentially fruitless. . . ." One cannot resist thinking here of the "fruitless" U.S. imperialism in Latin American "banana republics." He pays homage, commendably, to nineteenth-century anti-imperialists who warned against American conquest in the Caribbean and the Philippines and counsels that ecological limits have brought the U.S. empire into decline, sadly acknowledging, "We did not recognize precedents in time to avoid the frustration of ill-founded aspirations."

But there are those among us who celebrate and would like to participate more fully in the collapse of this and every empire, in order to find our way back to the harmonious relation with nature so longed for by deep ecologists. That this book has elicited such an enthusiastic response from them is disappointing, reflecting their serious political ignorance and conservative reaction to imperial decline. If anything, they should have noticed the connection between empire and habitat devastation, from ancient times to the carpet-bombing and defoliation of Indochina. Why is deep ecology so superficial when it comes to an analysis of contemporary empire, its origins and history?

An Economistic Analysis

In the economistic manner of Social Darwinism, Catton turns the natural world into a savings bank, yet he ignores global capitalism itself. So, for example, the collapse of the German economy after World War I, the Great Depression, and even the oil shortages of the 1970s were the result of natural scarcity and "carrying capacity deficit," rather than economic fluctuations (though ultimately real shortages of nonrenewable materials are inevitable). Manipulating a host of statistics, he explains that if current agriculture were to revert to preindustrial forms, *"four earths* would be needed" to support the present population. The rising use of copper, steel, and aluminum are also examples of "draw down" to extract needed phantom carrying capacity to support the population. In another tortured mathematical argument, we are told that in 1970 U.S. energy use amounted to 58 barrels of oil per capita annually. By strenuous calculation, he demonstrates that were we to try to get this energy from renewable, agricultural sources, rather than "phantom carrying capacity" of fossil fuels, we could get only 1.27 percent of current U.S. energy consumption. After this long exegesis, he concludes, "It should be clear, therefore, that the actual population of the United States [has] already overshot its carrying capacity measured by the energy-producing capability of visible American acreage."

But of course it is not so clear at all. If carrying capacity has been exceeded and there isn't enough to go around, why are crops systematically dumped and destroyed? Only a critique of the system that turns food into a commodity can make sense in such a context. And his numerical mystification fails to note that "per capita" energy consumption includes the urban megalopolises, the glut of industry, transport, the military, and the frenetic form of life specific to industrial capitalism. To identify biological carrying capacity with such figures is patently absurd.

There is no doubt that the present form of existence is destructive, and increasingly destructive as population grows. But to argue that "even our most normal and non-reprehensible ways of using resources to support human life and pursue human happiness" are destroying the environment is to forget that it is the form of culture in industrialism and the manner in which pursuing "life and happiness" is organized that is destroying life, not necessarily sheer population numbers. The toxic wastes produced by industrialism are not "unavoidably created by our life processes," they are the result of capitalist looting and a pathological culture. People need neither vast energy consumption nor toxic-waste production to be kept alive; in fact, we are being steadily poisoned by them.

The notion of carrying capacity is trivialized by reduction to absurd statistics. No one really knows what the earth's actual carrying capacity is, or how much land we need in order to live in a renewable manner. What have megatechnic projects, freeways, asbestos, nuclear power, armaments production, or the automobile to do with biological carrying capacity? What have they to do with anything except the inertia of investment, technological drift, and capital accumulation? Catton's ecological paradigm reduces everything to numbers and mechanistically applies its analysis to society, rendering it blind to the actual forces leading to extinction. When this methodology compares, for example, statist wars and imperial rivalry to the territorialism of animals, it imposes the (current) scientific description of one highly complex order onto another, unrelated one. This is pseudozoology at its worst.

Technology and Alienation

Catton's discussion also misapprehends the critical role of technology in the present crisis for all the same reasons (though it is not entirely devoid of insight or thoughtful observation). Catton follows the standard line of reasoning (so brilliantly discredited by Lewis Mumford in the early chapters of *The Myth of the Machine*) that sees human species-essence as that of a tool-using or "prosthetic" animal. In general, he confuses tools and tool use with the technological system. So, for example, seeing clothing (like all tools) as a prosthesis, he decides that central heating and air conditioning in modern buildings are simply extensions of clothing. His conclusion is thus predictable, and conforms to the standard ideology of technology: "If the digging stick was a prosthetic device, so was the modern power shovel."

This myopia discerns no difference between living in a hut or pueblo and a mega-high-rise, or between a spear and a missile, confusing the similarities between such phenomena and their far more important distinctions. It is beyond the scope of this essay to discuss the fallacy in detail, [6] but the metaphor of all technics as prostheses misses the qualitative transformation that occurs as technology becomes a system that envelops human beings and society, modifying their natures to conform to its operational demands.

When, for example, he employs the prosthesis metaphor to describe a pilot strapping a jet airplane to his waist, Catton forgets that the pilot becomes totally enclosed in an artificial environment and utterly dependent upon a technological system — all of it the crystallization of coerced labor, hierarchic domination, remote control, and alienation. For the same reason he misunderstands work, describing the technological and economic division of labor (in an uncanny inversion of Darwin's industrialized model of complex organisms) as "functionally equivalent to the interactions of diverse species." But these "biotic niches" are only positions in a social hierarchy, a work pyramid — the perfect definition of civilization.

Because its devastation is self-evident, Catton understands progress as "a disease." But he only seems to think so because it contaminates the habitat, forgetting that it contaminates the human spirit as well. "The more colossal man's tool kit became," he writes, "the larger man became, and the more destructive of his own future." There is no recognition in this formulation of alienation and the fundamental desire to cease being a thing among things, to become once more an integrated living being in an animate world. The more colossal technology has become, the smaller the individuals imprisoned within it, and the more suffocated and crushed by the artificial world built by their forced labor. *This* anguished condition is the authentic source of revolutionary change that will put an end to industrialism, rather than a scientific paradigm of energy exchanges between organisms and environment (which in any case has now been recognized by biotechnological capital as the basis for its further conquest of nature).

Scientific Ideology as Material Force

It follows that Catton's view of radical revolt is very negative. He has little sympathy for anticolonial movements, and even though it was during the 1960s (that "crescendo of ugly, mindless, and malicious behavior") that an environmental and anti-industrial awareness was renewed, he can only compare the radicalism of the period to "queue-jumping," a panic response, even to Nazism. His monolithic interpretation attributes all of these responses, of course, to population pressure. Rejection of the corporate state and a reorientation toward nature are criticized as superficial unless they are founded on an understanding of "geochemical processes" and resource limits. Radicals seek a "magic recipe for avoiding crash," he argues, and slogans like "Stop the bombing now!", "Freedom now!", and "End apartheid now!" (his list), as well as the "theft and publication of secret documents" (presumably the Pentagon Papers) and "the burning of flags and embassies" are only destructive panic responses and "queue-jumping." Even peace movements are to blame for missing "the environmental sources of antagonism."

His alternative is one of "enlightened self-restraint" and further inquiry (presumably in orderly lines behind politicians, scientists, and academics). He rejects "rampant competitiveness" while forgetting that the image of such competitiveness pervades his whole portrayal of nature. His proposals are few and tame: "ecological modesty," phasing out fossil fuels, a reform of the mass media, and a defense of existing environmental laws. Society must act "as if . . . we had already overshot," he writes, in a subtle softening of his thesis, and the crash must be ameliorated to save as many human lives as possible by a conscious renunciation of destructive industrialism and its culture.

His conclusions avoid advocating the die-off that his thesis suggests is inevitable. "Bankruptcy proceedings" must be held "against industrial civilization, and *perhaps* against the standing crop of human flesh," he argues, and in another modification he says, "There *might be* already too many of us" to return to a simpler, renewable life (my emphasis in both quotes — G.B.). He even warns that his method will not point to "obvious solutions to the predicament." Perhaps he perceives, if dimly, that scientific ideology becomes a material force with consequences. Social Darwinism, combined with eugenics (the genetic "control" and "improvement" of breeds), was employed to justify colonial conquest and to legitimate reactionary immigration policies around the turn of the century, and even led ultimately to eugenics-based extermination of psychiatric inmates, Jews, Gypsies, and other "subhuman breeds" by Nazi technocrats in their death camps. Today, overpopulation theories are used by development-bank bureaucrats to justify industrial development of sensitive wilderness areas (as in northern Brazil), and economic planners are currently utilizing "triage" analysis (a battlefield medical operation in which certain of the wounded are left to die in order to concentrate on those with a better chance of surviving) to consign masses of Third World peoples to starvation for the purposes of restructuring capital and paying off the national debts of countries like Mexico and Chile.

The Grasshopper and the Ant

Catton at least has the decency to distance himself a bit in his conclusions, seeking to avoid the "cruel genocide" that they imply by searching for an ecological reorientation and attempting to spare human life. There are others in the ecology movement who share the Malthusian premises of his flimsy "overshoot" thesis and who *embrace* such genocide — for others, that is. One prominent example is right-wing biologist Garrett Hardin (published in the Tobias anthology, though he is not in agreement with radical environmentalism). Hardin's zero-sum view of nature identifies bourgeois property rights with natural law: only private-property rights will protect the environment since treating nature as a shared "commons" will lead some to act irresponsibly and others to suffer for it. He argues, in true Malthusian neoconservative form, that "excessive altruism" (identified with liberalism and Marxism, of course) will plunge all, rich and poor, powerful and weak, "into the Malthusian depths."

Proposing instead a "lifeboat ethics," Hardin's theory is merely a repeat of the fable of the grasshopper and the ant, with a tinge of imperial hubris. While profligate and "over-fertile" Third World grasshoppers have "ruinously exploited" their environment, hard-working Euramerican ants have built their fortune and future. Now the hapless grasshoppers are swimming around the lifeboats of the wealthy nations, begging for admittance or a handout. But helping them will only eventually swamp the boats. "Comparable justice, complete catastrophe." An elegant parable. Hardin prefers instead "population control the crude way," and "reluctantly" suggests borders be closed, since "American women" would be rapidly surpassed in reproduction by immigrants. [7] In the Tobias anthology Hardin argues the impossibility of internationalism, proposing national patriotism as an alternative, stating, "there must be the patriotic will to protect what has been achieved against demands for a world-wide, promiscuous sharing." The nation "must defend the integrity of its borders or succumb into chaos."

Of course Hardin's "theory" only distills the diminished, crackpot outlook of free-market ideology and imperial arrogance, since the wealthy nations made themselves so by systematically looting not only the heritage of their own peoples but particularly the riches of the Third World. His "solutions" are the virus itself. But they are acceptable to many ecologists, who, according to Devall and Sessions, "argue that it is sometimes tactically wise to use the themes of nationalism or energy security to win political campaigns." It is a view held as well by the KKK, which (less reluctantly) has sent armed patrols to the U.S.-Mexico border to prevent Latin Americans from entering "illegally."

This patriotic nationalist fervor and aversion to Hispanics was also shared by the late novelist Edward Abbey (*éminence grise* and guru of the Earth First! group), who (from the formerly Mexican territory of southern Arizona) wrote in a letter printed in the April-May 1986 issue of *The Bloomsbury Review*: "In fact, the immigration issue really is a matter of 'we' versus 'they' or 'us' versus 'them.' What else can it be? There are many good reasons, any one sufficient, to call a halt to further immigration (whether legal or illegal) into the U.S. One seldom mentioned, however, is cultural: the United States that we live in today, with its traditions and ideals, however imperfectly realized, is a product of northern European civilization. If we allow our country — *our* country — to become Latinized, in whole or in part, we shall see it tend toward a culture more like that of Mexico. In other words, we will be forced to accept a more rigid class system, a patron style of politics, less democracy and more oligarchy, a fear and hatred of the natural world, a densely overpopulated land base, a less efficient and far more corrupt economy, and a greater reliance on crime and violence as normal instruments of social change." The contrast drawn between the U.S. and Mexico by this self-proclaimed "anarchist" is astonishing on several counts, any one sufficient to reveal his utter racism and historical stupidity. One might mention in passing the relationship between the corruption of the Mexican economy and U.S. economic domination (why, for one small example, U.S. companies and their subsidiaries can pollute and ravage the land and people with impunity there). Or perhaps we should consider the great love of nature he attributes to the North Americans, the absence here of oligarchic control, the "efficient economy." And, of course, "we" don't rely on crime and violence to effect political policy (as in Nicaragua, El Salvador, Guatemala). Abbey should have been ashamed, but he wasn't; he had a following.

A Deep Ecologist Who Advocates Genocide

Among his following are many of the eco-activists and deep ecologists of Earth First!, including their apparent leader, Dave Foreman, who in an interview with Bill Devall in the Australian magazine *Simply Living* said, regarding starvation in Ethiopia, that "the best thing would be to just let nature seek its own balance, to let the people there just starve. . . . " Giving aid would of course only spur the Malthusian cycle, thus "what's going to happen in ten years time is that twice as many people will suffer and die." Notice how Malthusian brutality is couched in the terms of humanitarian concern.

"Likewise," he said, "letting the USA be an overflow valve for problems in Latin America is not solving a thing. It's just putting more pressure on the resources we have in the USA. . . and it isn't helping the problems in Latin America." Notice here how rapidly the "anti-anthropocentrist" reverts to a nationalist resource manager. But his entire formulation, like those of Abbey and Hardin, reverses social reality and conceals the real sources of hunger, resource pressures, and refugees.

Central America is being devastated by U.S. corporate exploitation and a genocidal war to make sure the plunder continues. One horrible example is the U.S.-caused war in El Salvador, defending a death-squad government that would likely collapse in weeks without U.S. backing. The war has forced one quarter of the Salvadoran population to become refugees, and a half-million of them have fled to the U.S. Comments like Foreman's might not be quite so obscene if there were consistent coverage in his newspaper of U.S. exploitation in Central America (apart from the occasional material on rainforests, usually in a Rainforest Action Network supplement) and denunciations of the U.S. annihilation of the Salvadoran people, cultures, and lands, but there is no antiwar component in the paper and little about these interrelated problems in Central America. Foreman, too, ought to be utterly ashamed, but Foreman, too, has a following.

When Devall asked Foreman why the mainstream environmental movement had not addressed the population issue, the reply was, "you can't get any reaction." Foreman appeared to be implying that no serious dialogue could be generated on it, but if so, he was being less than candid. In the summer of 1986 I sent a friendly but critical letter to *Earth First!* which criticized contemporary Malthusianism and warned them to "not make the mistake of *advocating* the genocide that the industrial system is already carrying out." It was never printed, nor did it receive any response, though in subsequent issues Foreman stressed the need for an exchange of ideas and diverse points of view, describing the paper as "a forum of the deep ecology/Earth First! movement." [8]

I sent another letter questioning why mine was never printed, pointing out the problems with Foreman's comments on immigration and Ethiopia, and warning Earth First! to avoid becoming "vanguardist" by suppressing the diverse views it claims to want and which undoubtedly exist within the deep-ecology current. I finally received a note from Foreman himself, groaning, "Gawd, I'm bored with left-wing humanist rhetoric." In answer to my question about open discussion on the population issue, he replied, "My honest feeling is that the vast majority of those who consider themselves Earth First!ers agree with my position. . . . I am all for cooperation with other groups where it fits, but we have a particular point of view which we are trying to articulate. Call it fascist if you like, but I am more interested in bears, rainforests, and whales than in people."

Well, it's certainly Foreman's business to print, or not print, whatever he likes. And since I have access to publications myself, I gave up attempting an open and egalitarian discussion with him and decided to research deep ecology and the hunger question further. It was later that his comments on Ethiopia and related issues came to my attention, but they heightened my sense of unease with the direct-action environmental group that had previously earned my respect and praise in the *Fifth Estate*.

While Foreman's presumptuousness about speaking for the "vast majority" of Earth First! (and by extension, deep ecologists and even *other species*) is only manipulation, his acceptance of the fascist label is telling. There *is* a definite connection between fascism and his perception of world corporate genocide as nature taking its course. It is also fascistic to call for an end to immigration and the closing of borders, especially to exclude those who are fleeing a war waged by one's own country. (Perhaps Earth First! will volunteer to help round up those courageous people in the Sanctuary movement who, in the best tradition of the antislavery underground railroad, are aiding the refugees. Or they can help the KKK apprehend Guatemalan Indians, an animist, land-based people, fleeing a holocaust perpetrated with the active involvement of the U.S.) And, finally, smearing all anticapitalism or critiques of global corporate empire as "an ossified leftist worldview that blames everything on the corporations" (as Foreman does in the March 1987 *Earth First!*) is reminiscent of the anticommunist pseudoradicalism of the Nazis themselves. Certainly, "capitalists are not the only problem" (Foreman, in the June 1987 *Earth First!*). But Foreman should realize that the problem won't be resolved as long as capital exists. To deny the connection between chopping down trees and chopping down peasants is to show willful ignorance and to act in silent complicity with murderers. [9]

The Tattered Food-Web

The entire question of food is integral to deep ecology because food is essential to life. As Gary Snyder writes in the Sessions/Devall anthology, "The shimmering food-chain, food-web, is the scary, beautiful condition of the biosphere. . . . Eating is truly a sacrament." Anti-Malthusian and Malthusian will agree that the food-web is now in tatters. Agriculture is now a destructive industry, and people are going hungry in enormous numbers. Everyone agrees that fundamental imbalances underlie this situation. But what are they?

Foreman argues (in his interview with Devall) that "domesticating plants and animals is *violence* of the *worst* kind because it twists their natural evolutionary potential." Only a return to hunting-gathering and the die-off of the vast majority of people will bring things back into balance. Even gardening is a "violent activity." This viewpoint is not much of an option for the majority of us, and it's hardly going to be pursued. (In any case it is the old alienated dualism operating, that denies humans any place in nature, denies what we have evolved into; it's like decrying the mammals for eating dinosaur eggs. I am reminded of Kirkpatrick Sale's droll comment in *Human Scale* that "one must not, after all, confuse the ecological ideal of living *within* nature with the more Eastern notion, recently popular here among the hair-shirt wing of the back-to-nature people, of living *under* it."

The deep-ecologist argument, based on Catton's carrying-capacity theory, is that there is no longer enough to go around in anything resembling a renewable, sustainable manner. Any suspicion that starvation might presently be the result of distribution and other social conflicts alone, rather than natural limits, is considered a "humanist," "anthropocentric" (and probably Marxist) fantasy. (Perhaps other deep ecologists, such as Arne Naess, would not agree with such views, but few if any have criticized them or explicitly and forcefully distanced themselves from them.)

The population question is a numbers game, with many variables and many possible interpretations, as a perusal of the literature will confirm. Population has skyrocketed in the last few centuries. In the last century world population has more than doubled and has just hit the five-billion mark. The growth in the birth rate peaked between 1960 and 1965 and has been slowly falling. In 1980 it was about 2.17 percent and is expected to decline to about 1.84 percent by the year 2000. Growth in developed countries has been slowly grinding to a halt, which means that by the end of the century, when we reach six billion, five billion will be in the Third World.

The world-population growth rate has been declining even more than was previously expected, but nevertheless, population is still rising in overall numbers, from about 76 million a year at the present time to an expected 93 million at the century's end. One demographic forecast is that "if the world could reach replacement-level fertility by the year 2000, the world's population would stabilize at around eight and a half billion towards the year 2100." As Paul Harrison observes in his book *Inside the Third World* (Penguin, 1982), this means "that timing, in the battle to beat population growth, is of the essence," since the longer population stabilization takes, the higher population will be down the line.

Harrison describes the population growth as a result of the decline in the death rate rather than of a boom in the birth rate, which is actually declining overall, though much more slowly than the death rate. As the birth rate slows, it should eventually catch up with the death-rate decline, but it could take a good century or more in the Third World. There is some hope in the fact that the birth rate is slowing down even while the population in the Third World is actually much younger than before, but the overall picture is not encouraging.

"All the threats to the land, with the possible exception of salinization, are caused by poverty and overpopulation," writes Harrison, "and, in turn, they accentuate poverty." His book is a bleak picture of the state of the Third World and its implications for all of us. "Man and the land in poor countries are locked in a destructive and seemingly inescapable relationship, in which they are spiralling down, in self-fuelling motion, towards mutual destruction." The loss of land appears to be the main cause for the undermining of overall well-being — "the dispossession of small holders, increasing landlessness, mechanization, increasing population" all go together. What is happening in the Third World today seems to parallel the industrialization of Europe, which went through dispossession, landlessness, and population growth. But this time the consequences are further down the spiral for the whole world.

And yet Harrison still maintains that the entire crisis could at least have been lessened, "first and foremost by radical land reform and the establishment of cooperatives, giving everyone who lives on the land access to the land and its produce." Harrison is no *zapatista* or agrarian revolutionary, but he recognizes the need to promote subsistence, equity in resources, and basic health. In most countries, though, "government policies have been the direct opposite," and land reform has been either corrupted or a cover for the actual undermining of subsistence.

"There is really no such thing as world hunger," Harrison observes, "but only hunger of particular social groups. The total food resources available in the world would be perfectly adequate to feed everyone properly if they were fairly distributed among nations and social groups." This is Kirkpatrick Sale's argument in *Human Scale*, that there is more than enough to go around, and that "there is not a single country to which the U.S. exports grains that could not grow those grains itself." This view is also held by Frances Moore Lappé and Joseph Collins, whose 1978 book *Food First: Beyond the Myth of Scarcity* (dismissed as "absurd" in a one-liner by Foreman) is perhaps the most sophisticated anti-Malthusian argument available.

Despite some shortcomings in their views (a marked social-democratic, pro-development stance, and a lack of criticality concerning industrialism as a system and socialist countries like China, in particular), their arguments are very persuasive and bring together a critique of industrial agriculture and the global market that would help deep ecologists to ask deeper questions about hunger. [10] The notion that present scarcity is generated by overpopulation cannot be substantiated, they argue; not that there are no natural limits, but that "the earth's natural limits are not to blame." The world is presently producing enough grain to supply everyone's caloric and protein needs. (A third of it goes to livestock.) And these figures do not include the many other nutritious foods available, such as beans, nuts, fruits, vegetables, root crops, and grass-fed meat. The Malthusian argument "is worse than a distortion," they argue, since it shifts the blame to "natural limits" and to the hungry in a world where "surplus" food stocks are dumped like any other commodity to increase their profitability. Boring, left-wing humanism notwithstanding, the refusal to understand that food has become a commodity is to mystify the modern shredding of the sacred food-web.

The Global Supermarket

What are the causes of hunger? We should remember that, historically, colonialism, bringing with it an emerging capitalist economy and the wage system, destroyed the traditional economies in most countries. By substituting cash crops and monoculture for forms of sustainable agriculture, it destroyed the basic land skills of the people whom it reduced to plantation workers. With the traumatic destruction of indigenous cultures came a desperate acceptance of and desire for the industrialized goods of Western commodity society. Contrived by colonialism, this recipe for disaster accounts for the world crisis we are now witnessing.

Today, powerlessness over their lives and land is leading the people of the Third World to hunger and despair. Large landholders control the vast majority of the land in poor countries (and rich ones as well). They are also the least productive farmers. In 83 countries some three percent of landholders control 79 percent of all farmland. Their yields are lower, consistently so, than those of small landowners. Much of their land is left unplanted and is held to keep others from using it to compete on the market. A Colombian study in 1960 showed that the largest landholders, in control of 70 percent of the land, planted only six percent of their land. Peasants driven from the land by large landholders, as in Central America and particularly El Salvador, are driven up the mountain sides onto infertile lands where, to eke out a living, they cause erosion and generalized degradation of the land. When they try to regain their lands, they are shot down either by paid mercenaries or the official army and police. Or they flee to the cities and thus aggravate the problem of urbanization.

In Kenya in 1970, "3,175 large farms owned by Europeans, individual Africans, corporations, and some cooperatives, occupied 2.69 million hectares of the best land, while the country's 777,000 smallholders were crowded into only 2.65 million hectares," Harrison reports. "Even among the latter there were great disparities: the 52 percent with farms below two hectares occupied only 15 percent of the land, while the top 7 percent took up more than a third of the total." Kenya exports cotton, tea, tobacco, coffee, and (Del Monte) pineapples, while its people go hungry. Privatizing land holding and destroying older traditions of community mutualism has undermined subsistence throughout Africa and Asia. As a U.N. report on the conditions of the Sahel (Mauritania, Mali, Niger, and Chad) states, "All it now takes is a year or two of short rain and what is left lands in the hands of a few individuals." Drought in Africa was part of a millennia-long cycle. But it was cash-crop exploitation, a market economy, and taxation that led to starvation there rather than drought. "Ships in the Dakar port bringing in 'relief' food (during the hunger crisis in the 1970s) departed with stores of peanuts, cotton, vegetables, and meats," write Lappé and Collins. "Of the hundreds of millions of dollars' worth of agricultural goods the Sahel exported during the drought, over 60 percent went to consumers in Europe and North America and the rest to the elites in other African countries." In Chad an *increase* in cotton production went hand in hand with mass hunger. The increase in cotton production throughout the Sahel led a French nutritionist to remark, "If people were starving, it was not for lack of cotton."

Harrison's study confirms Lappé and Collins's argument. "Much of the best land that should be used for domestic food production in the developing countries is growing cash crops for the West," he writes, and "five of the most common, sugar, tobacco, coffee, cocoa, and tea, are not doing the West much good either." Cattle production for consumption by the imperial metropolises also undermines local subsistence, Harrison observes. "'Sheep eat men,' the peasants displaced by enclosures of common land in England used to complain. Cash crops eat men in much of the developing world."

Even during the 1973-74 hunger crisis there was no shortage of food, according to Sale. In Bangladesh, frequently referred to as the model for the Malthusian overpopulation argument (and where 90 percent of the land is worked by sharecroppers and laborers), many people starved after the 1974 floods while hoarders stacked up four million tons of rice because the majority was too poor to buy it. The cash crops themselves bring currency or goods into agro-exporting countries, but this money goes to buy industrial-consumer goods like refrigerators, air conditioners, cars, and refined foods for the elites, as well as to pay for a booming arms race (mostly to repress their own populations). Multinationals, meanwhile, are now taking at least seven billion dollars a year more from the Third World in official payments than they are putting back in, "and probably a good deal more via transfer payments." notes Harrison. [11]

Cash crops go to feed the global supermarket, particularly in the metropolis, and yield huge profits for international capital to industrialize the planet. [12] Mexican soil and labor are already supplying one-half to two-thirds of the U.S. market for many winter and early-spring vegetables. The shift from local consumption to production for export to the U.S. is astonishing. In operations mostly financed and contracted by U.S. corporations, from 1960 to 1976 onion imports to the U.S. increased over five times to 95 million pounds; cucumber imports went from under nine million pounds to 196 million pounds. From 1960 to 1972 eggplant imports multiplied ten times, squash 43 times. Frozen strawberries and cantaloupe from Mexico represent a third of U.S. annual consumption, and about half of the winter tomatoes sold here are Mexican. Meanwhile, agriculture for local consumption is being squeezed out, raising prices of basic staples.

One third to one half of total meat production in Central America and the Dominican Republic is exported, principally to the U.S. In Costa Rica meat consumption declined as exports to the U.S. grew, much of it going to fast-food hamburgers. [13] Guatemala, Ecuador, and to some extent Mexico are being turned into major flower exporters for the global supermarket. Brazil has increased production of soybeans (to be fed to American and Japanese livestock) by more than twentyfold in the last decade, Sale reports, "while its production of food crops has already declined." In northeast Brazil, according to Harrison, "dense stands of thick green sugar cane wave their silvery tassels in the breeze, while the laborers who plant and cut it are squeezed onto the roadsides in their little huts and have no room for even a few vegetables. [14]

In this scenario not even increased food production serves

to help the hungry. As Lappé and Collins demonstrate, "the increase in poverty has been associated not with a fall but with a rise in cereal production per head, the main component of the diet of the poor." So the image of Green Revolution technology (drawn for example by Catton) as causing a population increase and subsequent destruction of carrying capacity is a fiction. The Green Revolution is utilized by large landholders to produce for the global supermarket, not to feed people locally. It *increases* hunger by bringing the industrial revolution to agriculture, thus destroying subsistence as well as agricultural and genetic diversity, and by creating dependence on chemical fertilizers, pesticides, and machinery — and the corporations that produce them.

Nor is toxic-chemical agriculture a result of population pressure. The U.S. uses one billion pounds of toxic pesticides, herbicides, and fungicides annually — some 30 percent of world consumption. A good part of the applications are simply for cosmetic purposes, with as much as a third going to golf courses, lawns, parks, and gardens. Lappé and Collins estimate that, despite a tenfold increase in the use of such agents, the crop loss to pests in this country has remained at around 30 percent since the 1940s. They argue that if such chemicals were eliminated altogether, losses would increase by about only 7 percent. In the meantime, in addition to the ecological destruction pesticides bring about, their residues are considered by the Environmental Protection Agency to be "the nation's third worst environmental cancer risk after toxic chemicals in the workplace and radon gas in the home." [15] Half of all pesticides produced, some of them illegal in the U.S., go to the Third World, but they come back to haunt us with our morning coffee and cantaloupe.

So toxic agriculture is not a function of subsistence but of corporate profits. To link the two in a Malthusian argument is to line up indirectly with the *Wall Street Journal*, which argued that the disaster at Bhopal was unfortunate but a necessary risk in order to feed people. Bhopal wasn't only a horrifying example of a technological civilization completely out of control, it was a corporate crime. It is those sorcerer's apprentices, the capitalist corporations, we might remind these careless deep ecologists, who turn scarcity and starvation in one place into luxuries somewhere else. And where people resist the operations of this "economic freedom," the armed might of the state, complete with covert and overt operators, steps in to make sure that things remain just as they are and that business goes on as usual.

Under increasing attack, squeezed from all sides, the world's poor are having large families in a desperate attempt to get support in their old age, to obtain cheap labor power on their plots or in the labor market, and to overcome high infant-mortality rates. In much of the world, another child is an economic benefit and will bring more income to the family than will be expended in the child's upkeep. [16] Yet there are also many indications that large families have an adverse effect on their members, who tend to be less nourished and in worse health than those of smaller families. Furthermore, as Harrison observes, this short-term survival strategy has long-term social costs for the community and the country in land fragmentation, erosion, poverty, and urbanization. The poor of the Third World are courting "long-term ruin to avoid immediate disaster."

The World Going to Hell

Whatever the basis of analysis, the prospects are indeed grim. One cannot help but agree with Catton's statement, "The time may be near when it will take an optimist to believe the future is uncertain." The world is going to hell. And the optimism that might be found among certain investment strategists and technocrats is anything but reassuring. Industrialization continues unabated in its frenzied obliteration of life. Harrison sees overpopulation as one of several interlocking factors causing the present growing world crisis, and remarks that Malthus may yet have his say. "If a non-oil agricultural practice is not developed fast," he writes, "available food per capita will start to decline. . . . If man does not conquer the population problem, nature will step in and do it for him." The Food First thesis supports the goal of a stabilized population but sees the population pressure more as a "symptom and aggravating factor" in the crisis. While these interpretations vary, their recommendations are similar.

Both views see a renewal of local subsistence and self-reliance as key, and both call for radical, sweeping land reform. This does not mean a simple redistribution, however, but the creation of cooperative, participatory, and egalitarian societies aimed at helping the people at the very bottom. Lappé and Collins write that their perspective "is not a simple call to put food into hungry mouths." In fact, they oppose food aid because it does not reach the hungry, undermines revolt, and destroys local food production. They insist, rather, that "if enabling people to feed themselves is to be the priority, then all social relationships must be reconstructed." This amounts to a call for agrarian revolution.

First and foremost, such a revolution must liberate women. They are "the poorest of the poor," as Harrison says. They constitute "the largest group of landless laborers in the world," since even in cooperatives and land redistributions, they are frequently shut out. Industrialization and urbanization also hurt them the most, destroying their handicrafts and worsening the unjust division of labor to "the notorious double day" of wage work and household work. If they have fewer children, they suffer for lack of labor power; if they have more, they are overburdened and their health undermined.

The population question can never be addressed until having fewer children can become a reasonable option. That means freedom for women from male domination, and an agrarian social transformation that reunites agriculture and nutrition, renews self-reliance and subsistence, and creates equality. If deep ecologists can recognize that these social questions must be resolved in order to reconcile humanity with the natural world, that a whole earth vision must be grounded in the social, they will make the leap that they desire in their understanding and practice. Human liberation is integrally bound up with the liberation of nature, and therefore is truly "deep ecological."

It is a tenet of deep ecology that nature is "more complex than we can possibly know" (Sessions and Devall). In that case, deep ecologists should refrain from blanket statements about human populations, since no interpretation can presently be substantiated in any absolute terms. (So glib remarks about someone else's "die-off" only come from a *preference*, not a recognition of natural necessity. In such a case "theory" is nothing but mean-spirited ideology, with fascist implications — and helps, by the way, neither bears nor whales nor rainforests.) Catton says there are already too many people; Sale, on the other hand, argues that the entire world's population could fit into the U.S. with a density less than England's, and in the fertile agricultural regions with a density like that of Malta. The statistics, to back up arguments, grow exponentially.

Meanwhile, practical steps must be taken to stop the process by which the world and everything in it are being reduced to money, and finally, to toxic waste. "Letting nature take its course" by consigning people to starvation is not a solution even within its own terms, since the deteriorating situation described so vividly by Harrison and others won't go away when a few million — or many millions — die. The earth will continue to be gouged and the forests leveled, and society's capacity to bring about change will be diminished. Such Malthusianism even violates deep ecology, since it neglects the totality of the habitat destroyed for all species in the wake of the famine and doesn't recognize that environmental desolation in one place affects natural integrity everywhere.

In *The Conquest of Bread*, Peter Kropotkin raised the issue that remains central today for social and ecological transformation. Bread, he said, "must be found for the people of the Revolution, and the question of bread must take precedence of all other questions. If it is settled in the interests of the people, the Revolution will be on the right road; for in solving the question of Bread we must accept the principle of equality, which will force itself upon us to the exclusion of every other solution." In answer to Kropotkin's profound observation, some among the deep ecologists would prefer to respond with a simple program: let them starve.

And perhaps they have a point. Perhaps there *are* too many people to live in a renewable manner. Perhaps the starvation of some is unavoidable. But as long as poor and tribal people around the globe starve while overfed, high-energy-consuming bankers sit in air-conditioned high-rises in New York, Paris, or Dakar, something is wrong. Before the poor of the world die of hunger — those little communities which are also small and unique parts of the whole picture, as Aldo Leopold might have said — let's deal with the neckties in the high-rises. It's nature's way too, after all, for people to pool their imaginations and their desires to cooperate in making revolutionary change.

Sessions and Devall write that "Certain outlooks on politics and public policy flow naturally" from ecological consciousness. This is manifestly untrue. Ecology, as I have shown, is an ambiguous outlook, and can lead in many directions. Deep ecology is layered, as is all scientific thinking about the social, with all the ideological compost and decay of a crumbling civilization about to collapse or devolve into something even more horrible. Deep ecology — starting from an intuition about the unity of life, an intuition of primal traditions present in the undercurrents of this civilization — claims to be a new paradigm, a philosophical and social system. This outlook enjoys increasing legitimacy in radical environmentalist circles as a coherent political perspective. Yet while deep ecology may draw from many profound sources in the long oral and written traditions of natural observation, there are many deep problems with the movement it has inspired.

Deep ecology loves all that is wild and free, so I share an affinity with deep ecologists that has made this essay difficult to write. I have written this detailed critique because I find it troubling and depressing that a movement so courageously and persistently involved with direct action to defend the earth can simultaneously exhibit reactionary, inhuman politics, and survivalist posturing. Deep ecologists, particularly Earth First!, have come to recognize the centrality of technology in the destruction of the earth. But if they remain blind to the interrelatedness of capital and the state with the planetary megatechnic work pyramid that is devouring nature, they will become mired in an elitist warrior survivalism that will lead nowhere.

As long as deep ecologists discern the present apocalyptic period as a result of a species-wide "biotic exuberance" in the imagery of bacteria, they will remain in a mystical domain of original sin, misanthropy, and Malthusian indifference to human suffering. This fatal error will not only serve to conceal the real structural sources of the present devastation — the system by which we all, dispossessed peasants and deep ecologists alike, court disaster by simply surviving in an increasingly constricted, deadened world — but will also undermine the chances for the human solidarity that might overcome it.

I believe that little by little (and perhaps already too late), people around the world are beginning to see these connections, to recognize that capital, technology, and the state are an interlocking, armored juggernaut that must be dismantled and overthrown if we are to renew a life in harmony with nature and human dignity. They are also increasingly aware that we cannot go on "living" like this, that we are sawing the branch out from underneath ourselves. The mystique of technological progress must be fought in city and country, defending habitat and halting the toxic production process.

We cannot isolate one bioregion or watershed from another — they are all part of one living organism. And we cannot separate fundamental human needs from those of the planet because they are consonant with one another, not opposed. So the changes that we all desire must occur deep down, at the level of human society, or nothing will prevent capital from utterly destroying nature as we know it. If an intransigently radical, visionary, earth-centered culture that fights for the earth is to flourish, radical environmentalism must confront its own ideological contradictions before they crystallize into a religion, complete with high priests and leaders, and squander what may be our last dwindling opportunities to stop this global megamachine and renew life.

Notes

[1] The mechanistic application of so-called natural laws to society impoverishes social critique. Deep-ecology articles are frequently rife with glib comparisons between humanity and "grey fuzz," lemmings, algae, and other species, followed by simplistic, almost Aesopian comments on complex issues specific to human society. One example is an article, "On Horns and Nukes" (*Earth First!*, September 1986), in which the author, George Wuerthner, blithely compares the current nuclear-arms race to the rivalry and "dominance hierarchy" of bighorn rams based on horn size. I'll leave aside his zoological interpretations, but given ecological science, there is much room for differences even there. The article's real absurdity is the idea that "nuclear weapons may not function primarily as offensive weapons, but like the horns of the Bighorn ram, may represent a nation's rank within the international community." Nothing here about the complex social relations that underlie nuclearism and the arms race, such as the original (offensive) use of nukes and their continuing use as a threat in making geopolitical policy. (See Daniel Ellsberg's enlightening introduction to Thompson and Smith's *Protest and Survive* for a brief history of the uses of the bomb.) Nothing about the massive technological bureaucracy, the permanent war economy, and the technological drift so brilliantly described by C.W. Mills, in *The Causes of World War Three*, back in the 1950s. Nothing about the Cold War and the militarization of culture, despite the wealth of information and the high-level sophistication of much of the antiwar and antinuclear movements in this country. No, because nuclear weapons systems (and their civilization) are just the horns of sheep (and nation-states the members of a bighorn "community"). Wuerthner wishes to avoid any "simplistic solution" to the problem, arguing: "Like the bull Elk who has lost his antlers, a direct reduction of nuclear stockpiles could destabilize the world's tenuously recognized hierarchy of military power. . . . Such a reduction may inadvertently bring us closer to nuclear war, rather than further away." This is Reagan talking to the disarmament movement, or James Watt, with peudoscience to back him up. What does our philosopher recommend? If horn-display is part of the problem, he says, "research by the U.S. government in human perceptions of status, rank, and power

might reveal a partial solution to the arms race." Perhaps the government will farm that study out to the Rand Corporation or one of the other think-tanks and let us know how it turns out. Meanwhile, such willful ignorance on this naturalist's part not only reflects the limitations of ecological ideology, but almost brings tears to one's eyes over the contradiction between the environmentalist concern for nature and its legitimation of the nuclear empire — this kind of silliness from a journal claiming to be at "the cutting edge" of this "new ecological paradigm."

[2]   As Dennis Wrong argues in *Population and Society* (1966), the capacity for population to surpass subsistence is undeniable, "but it leaves entirely open the question of the degree to which at a given time the capacity is actually being realized . . . for whenever a case is found in which the means of subsistence are abundant and population growth falls short of Malthus' maximum rate, by *definition*, the checks are at work preventing a more rapid increase."

Among many naturalists, the Malthusian proposition is not considered applicable to either human or animal populations. As D. H. Stott writes (in "Cultural and Natural Checks on Population Growth," in Andrew P. Vayda, *Environment and Cultural Behavior*, 1969), "That the amount of food available sets the ultimate limit to the growth of all animal and human populations cannot be disputed. But this apparently self-evident proposition only holds good in a very rough way over a long period. The popular Malthusian notion that the number surviving from year to year is determined by the current supply of food, with the excess dying from starvation, is no longer supported by any student of natural population." Utilizing many animal-population studies, including those of lemmings perennially used by Malthusians, Stott demonstrates that other built-in population-limiting factors occur that refute the Malthusian hypothesis, such as decreased viability of the young and infertility, even when food is available. There is evidence that human populations function similarly, according to Stott, hence the Malthusian catastrophe is "unlikely to occur," and will be avoided by complex limiting factors if not by conscious human intervention. In any case, the toxic contamination of human beings appears to be laying the basis for a population decline in the ugliest of terms.

The Malthusians might argue that while increased infertility and inviability of offspring is occurring among humans, medical technology is keeping alive people that would have died under natural conditions. They are certainly correct on this score, but they have missed the point. We must resist the medicalization of our lives because it is undermining our humanity with its insane premise to overcome all death and disease. We are going to have to relearn to live with death, which may mean letting die people whom technology keeps alive, if we are to avoid being drawn into a deepening technological control of life. Medicalization and its promise of overcoming death lead directly to bioengineering and the undermining and restructuring of human beings, which will bring us either to medico-technological catastrophe that wipes everything out, or an engineered Brave New World. Furthermore, the medical industry is itself a tremendous polluter, as the recent controversy over the low-level-radiation landfill to be constructed in Michigan attests. An enormous landfill must be built to store radioactive wastes — many of them medically generated — for several hundred years. So we see the irony of medical nuclear technology, used to cure diseases like cancer (when, in fact, little progress has been made on any of these fronts anyway), *causing* cancer, birth defects, and so on as it becomes a mountain of toxic residue. This must stop; with it, of course, will end certain short-term medical benefits (and a lot of medical exploitation of sick people and medically induced disease, as well). The few short-term benefits that medical high technology brings are outweighed by its long-term deleterious effects on nature and human health. The death rate, including that of infants, may rise as this shift occurs, which would work with other factors to bring down population, but this is still not at all a confirmation of the Malthusian view that there are too many people now on earth. This discussion demands more attention than a footnote; I am only raising the issue, not proposing to identify the exact point to which medicalization must be dismantled.

As an element of a rightward shift among some university circles, Malthusianism could be dusted off and relegitimated by scientists, but presently one can at least see that the population question, even among animal populations, is not clear-cut, and that there are still many differences of interpretation. Wrong notes that the decline in the rate of growth in the developed world severely undermines Malthusianism, and adds, "The natural sciences contribute significantly to the study of population. But the main causes of population trends, and the consequences of them that arouse great interest, are social." While an unlimited growth in population is indisputably a cause of human suffering, Wrong argues, "Malthus' view of human nature was that of a biological determinist."

3   Bill McCormick argues in "Towards an Integrated Approach to Population and Justice," in the August 1986 *Earth First!*, that "a dual approach" to population must be taken, reversing population trends while fighting economic injustice. Yet his argument rests on an attack on Frances Moore Lappé and Joseph Collins's *Food First* and its demonstration that only a struggle for economic justice will be effective in stabilizing populations. McCormick's approach starts from the assumption that "any modern social problem" must be considered by also "considering population density as a serious factor, not an insignificant one. . . ."

Nowhere does he refute *Food First*'s argument that population density is not a factor in present starvation (many starving countries have relatively low population densities, while countries with greater densities are self-sufficient or potentially self-sufficient) or that present hunger is not caused by overpopulation. While he agrees that a struggle for justice is key, his solution is a homily that "we" start having fewer children. In "Earth First versus Food First," in the Summer 1987 *Kick It Over* (P. O. Box 5811, Station A, Toronto, Ontario M5W 1P2 Canada), he repeats his argument, noting that the U.S. position under Reaganism followed the "resourceful earth" hypothesis of Julian Simon and Herman Kahn that is hostile to birth-control policies because, it argues, "continuous growth is good for the planet." While "Reagan Era" reactionaries do oppose birth control and abortion rights in the Third World with absurd economistic, technocratic, and moralistic arguments, they actually represent a variant of modern Malthusianism (Malthus also opposed birth control as immoral), since their arguments are linked to the opposition to social-welfare programs as well, based on arguments about the resolution of population and development crises by "free market" capitalist economics. For a critique of neoconservative Malthusians that suffers from a liberal technofix perspective on the problem of hunger, see "Malthus Then and Now" by John L. Hess, in the April 18, 1987 issue of *The Nation*. Jonathan Kieberson's article, "Too Many People?", in the June 26, 1986 *New York Review of Books*, also treats some recent neoconservative arguments. He notes as well that in many poor countries, "policies to alter reproductive behavior do not work well." While many factors may be involved, a central factor appears to be that "people do not wish to change their decisions to have many children." Clearly, social factors, many of them discussed in great detail by Lappé and Collins, underlie such decisions, so arguments like McCormick's are little better than sermons — sermons that tend to affirm the Malthusian legitimation of starvation even as they argue for social justice.

[4]   For example, William Vogt's 1948 *Road to Survival* called for strict population controls since there would be no time, as some argued, for populations to stabilize on their own. Why "ship food to keep alive ten million Indians and Chinese this year, so that fifty million may die five years hence," he mused. "China quite literally cannot feed more people. . . . There can be no way out. These men and women, boys and girls, must starve as tragic sacrifices on the twin altars of uncontrolled human reproduction and uncontrolled abuse of the land's resources."

This same kind of argument was advanced by another ecological writer, John Steward Collis, in *The Triumph of the Tree* (1954). This eminently civilized biocentric thinker writes of the "dread subject, this of population," that "In 1770 the vastly overpopulated continent of India was the victim of a famine in which ten million people died. That was excellent — as seen from the viewpoint of the animals. . . . But our approach is so extraordinary. We really seem to think that human beings should be exempt from natural laws."

[5]   Naturalist Gary Paul Nabhan relates some examples in an interview in the July/August 1986 issue of the Colorado literary magazine, the *Bloomsbury Review*, describing the gathering of "sandfood" (a dune plant endemic to the delta of the Colorado River) by the Sand Papago Indians. This human "takeover" reflects a natural *interaction* which

played a crucial role in the germination of the plant; in fact as gathering has declined, so have the plant's numbers. Another example is the parsnip of the Northwest: "The way it was gathered actually increased its vegetative propagation." This perspective is similar to Kropotkin's critique, in *Mutual Aid*, of nineteenth-century ideology and to many of the writings of renowned American naturalist Carl O. Sauer, who posed "ecological equilibrium" as an alternative to the Malthusian proposition which, as he argued, has never been proven. (See his *Selected Essays: 1964-1975*, from the Turtle Island Foundation, 1981.)

[6]   I have written about it already in "Technology: A System of Domination," the *Fifth Estate*, Winter 1984. (See also the related articles on technology in the Summer 1981 and Fall 1981 issues.)

[7]   In response to the suggestion that his recommendations might be racist, he counters with an example of Japanese-Americans trying to stop immigration to the Hawaiian Islands because of the severe limitations on land. This argument repelled me personally, for I have spent much time in the islands and have seen with my own eyes what the private property so hallowed in Hardin's view has done. It is not an abstract population question there; it is the runaway tourism development and the agro-industrial contamination that are Hawaii's problems. Hardin's article is "Lifeboat Ethics: The Case Against Helping the Poor," in *Psychology Today*, September 1974.

[8]   Actually, a tiny slice of my friendly *cover* letter was printed, where I took issue with Foreman's offhand comment in a previous issue that social ecologist Murray Bookchin "would do well to get out of his stuffy libraries and encounter the wilderness," calling it an irrelevant and unjust personal attack. Foreman printed this one remark, responding that his comment was "a fundamental critique of Bookchin and anyone else who relies excessively on scholarship instead of direct wilderness experience for wisdom." He added that "in virtually every area where I disagree with him, his lack of direct wilderness experience is the key. I do not believe that anyone, no matter how learned or thoughtful, can fully understand human society or the relationship of humans to the natural world without regularly encountering the wilderness and finding

instruction there." This, of course, is nothing but mystical demagogy. Foreman didn't get his ideas on Ethiopia, Latin America, deep ecology, or anything else directly from the wilderness, but from reading books and articles like everyone else — particularly, for one example, from Paul Shephard's strange and technocratic book, *The Tender Carnivore and the Sacred Game*, and for another, from David Ehrenfeld's *The Arrogance of Humanism*, which are both beyond the scope of this essay to review. It is demagogy as well because Foreman doesn't know about Bookchin's experience and because it implies that it is his own (presumably correct) wilderness "instruction" that tells him exactly where Bookchin's ideas go wrong. Foreman is claiming a special relationship with nature and using it to pontificate on political questions (like letting others starve). Whether any wilderness experience, even that of primal people, can be called "direct" is questionable. But the wilderness experience of anyone grown up in industrial civilization is *always* mediated by ideology and culture. "Direct wilderness experience" is also a middle-class fad, with an enormous industry in nylon and aluminum and plastic products to make it all possible. Foreman, after all, is no primal person coming from a culture embedded in the natural world; he is a frontiersman, a settler, who forgets that being in nature physically does not in and of itself promise any insight. As Hegel said of nomads, they bring their world with them. (*Simply Living*, in which the Foreman-Devall interview appeared, is a green-oriented magazine available from P. O. Box 704, Manly 2095, N. S. W., Australia.)

9   Foreman's views may have changed somewhat since this essay was written. When asked about the Malthusian position at a speaking engagement in Ann Arbor, Michigan in February 1989, he responded that Malthus was not entirely right, and that he himself had "no answers" to the population question. He is no longer editor of *Earth First!*, though he remains its publisher and the paper continues to publish Malthusian articles and to push Catton's book. (On the Earth First! bookstore page, always "annotated and introduced" by Foreman, he writes in the June 1988 and subsequent issues that Catton demonstrates that "we have indeed surpassed our carrying capacity," and, "If you believe the humanist bunk that Malthus is wrong, you definitely need to read it!"

A debate that occurred in *Earth First!* over the question of anarchy also points to the actual conservative discourse underlying much of the radical posturing of activists influenced by deep ecology. It began with an attack on anarchism in the May 1986 issue by writer Andrew Schmookler, author of *The Parable of the Tribes*, and described by editor Foreman as "one of the best ecological thinkers in the U.S." Schmookler's essay, sprinkled with parenthetical praise and advertisements for his book by the editor, argues against a more anarchist-oriented writer, Australopithecus, that the "unnatural condition of anarchy, far from being our salvation, has been at the root of the torment of civilization." The emergence of the state, in Schmookler's tired logic, is reason enough for anarchy to be rejected. "Anarchists want us to break up political powers, back to a multitude of small and self-governing communities," he writes. "But the human species tried that experiment — up until 10,000 years ago. And the rest is . . . history." The rest is history, of course, as it is commonly defined, but Schmookler fails to notice that the "experiment" lasted for 99 percent of human existence.

Given Schmookler's definition of anarchy as "action ungoverned by any lawful order" (chaos, in other words), his conclusions are foreordained. What existed before civilization's liquidation of the "experiment" of small, self-governing communities was *not* anarchy, he says. "True, there was no hierarchical power structure, but there was governing order. . . . There is no ruler in this lawful order. . . . Each follows only its own law — pursuing its own ends — but this law and these ends are part of a harmonious natural order." Schmookler is an ignoramus who hasn't even read a basic anthology of anarchist philosophy since he has more or less described anarchy as its classical proponents defined it. No hierarch, no leader (or archon), no archy or state: anarchy. He does not have the slightest idea what he is talking about. For him, anarchy is how the state and its ideologues, how hanging judges and newspaper headlines define it.

Hence his conclusion that "the state is but a symptom of the fundamental problem," which is power. Therefore, contradictorily, "power is necessary for social survival . . . we had better create sufficient government to control the free play of power . . . there should be a world order sufficient" to carry out this task. The state, a symptom of the problem of power, becomes the solution. In answer to the obvious response, who will guard the guardian, he solemnizes, "Government is a paradox, but there is no escaping it." This ecclesiastical line evokes an image of Winston Smith fleeing from the gaze of Big Brother, or Guy Debord's remark that this civilization "no longer promises anything. It no longer says, 'What appears is good, what is good appears.' It simply says: 'It is so.'"

Smugly extolling slave-owning colonial conquerors such as Madison and the framers of the U.S. Constitution, Schmookler asks, "Why do we send out the National Guard when a disaster disrupts society's order?" Society's "order" includes the business-as-usual of work slavery and ecological devastation that Earth First! and many others spend their time fighting, but no matter. And he posits the horrible situation in Lebanon as an example of what happens in the absence of a strong, centralized state. There were many responses to Schmookler from the Earth First! ranks and elsewhere; most were suppressed by the editors, though Schmookler had a chance to quote from some of them in order to answer his invisible critics. Three different people told us that they had responded, two of them Earth First!ers, but their letters never saw the light of day. One, Jack Straw (c/o *The Daily Battle*, 2000 Center Street #1200, Berkeley, CA 94704), replied to Schmookler that "Governors and presidents (not the abstract 'we' you refer to) send out the National Guard not to protect the many against the terrorist few, but to guard private property. . . . " All of this was lost on Schmookler, but the rank-and-file subscribers never got a chance to make up their own minds by reading different points of view.

The points of view they read were those of luminaries approved by the editor, particularly Edward Abbey, who blamed the slaughter in Lebanon on overpopulation and whose defense of anarchy sounded more like a portrait of vigilantism. Even regular contributor Christopher Manes, who accurately blamed the crisis in Lebanon not on statelessness but on the state, failed to point out the patterns of interimperial rivalry and the present role of the U.S. empire and its client state Israel in the unravelling and slaughter occurring throughout the Middle East. Again, the lack of an understanding (or at least an articulation) of the social-political context, even from the anarchist-oriented wing of Earth First!, is startling.

As for Schmookler, he is only a U.S. nationalist and a shill for authoritarian power. On Central America, for example, Schmookler wrote in the February 11, 1985 issue of *New Options* (in a piece entitled "Remember U.S. Interests") that "nations . . . do not have the luxury of being completely unselfish. . . . And it is not desirable for people of goodwill to debate U.S. foreign policy without regard to American interests." He admits that he does not know "what vital American interests are at stake in Central America," but he hypocritically asserts that the U.S. "plays an overall positive role" not only in the world, but "in the evolution of our species." Here, again, is the imperialist Darwin (and Spencer)! "The world would be a worse place," we are lectured, "if the United States disappeared overnight." He might ask the opinion of the 100,000 Guatemalans murdered by U.S.-backed dictatorships since the C.I.A. overthrow of their government in 1954, or the 50,000 Salvadorans butchered by another U.S. client, with U.S. support, since 1980, and on and on. But of course they can't reply. Schmookler decides that since the U.S. shouldn't disappear, we must understand that sometimes "our vital interests and the rights of others" may conflict, making necessary "agonizing moral choices." This is an apology for systematic genocide.

Foreman's touting of this "ecological thinker" seems to indicate not only a conservative, imperialist element among contemporary environmentalists, but a desire to head off the healthy, antiauthoritarian currents in the group that recognize the link between U.S. corporate empire, international imperialist conflict, the state, and the ecological crisis. But the "big guns" he employed were rather pitiful.

[10] One of the book's greatest shortcomings is probably its failure to address the problem of the rising aspirations in the Third World for a highly industrialized society, based on the same positivistic-scientistic religion that has led the Western world to the technological impasse it presently faces. Perhaps this was beyond the scope of a book which focused on discrediting the myths of world hunger, but industrialization and the industrialization of culture, from a social as well as an ecological point of view, are as serious threats as any other faced in the Third World. As Rudolf Bahro writes in *Socialism and Survival*, "On a world scale industrialization *cannot* be achieved any longer," since the earth's natural limits will not allow the growing world population to

live like the current North American middle class. "And at the national level industrialization can no longer solve any problems of *general* interest. As has been shown in the last decade — the so-called decade of development — industrialization will only increase the sum of absolute impoverishment. The conclusion is to disengage, not for a better industrialization, but for a different type of civilization. . . . " What should "the wretched of the earth . . . direct themselves towards?" Bahro asks. "Shouldn't the inhabitants of the *ranchos* organize for something very similar to the Old Testament exodus from Egypt: an outbreak back to the countryside?" The monster we face, therefore, is not simply plunder and inequitable distribution. "The monster is our industrial system, our industrial way of life itself." (*Socialism and Survival*, Heretic Books, 1982.)

[11]   Harrison comments that if one were to consider the idea of reparations to the Third World for exploitation and damage done, the total "would probably be astronomical." To give an idea, he mentions Chile. There, under the government of Salvador Allende, economists, deciding on compensation costs that would be paid to multinational corporations for nationalizing copper holdings, "estimated that the companies had made excess profits of $774 million and that far from having a right to any compensation, the companies actually owed Chile $378 million." Of course, the United States quickly put an end to this kind of economic speculation.

[12]   Actually, multinational corporations are attempting to shift the global supermarket in the Third World as well. India, for example, has a sizable modern economy and middle class with perhaps as many as 50 million people "who can consume on the level with most Americans and Western Europeans," according to one corporate advisor quoted by Lappé and Collins. Many multinationals are rapidly buying out and wrecking local food-producing concerns and pushing their high-energy-consuming, less nutritious products on the Third World. The distribution of food within Third World countries is as uneven as the discrepancies between them and the industrialized nations, and it is getting worse, as the figures in Harrison's book show.

[13] In Costa Rica, beef production nearly quadrupled between 1960 and 1980, but local consumption declined by almost 40 percent. "Guatemala and Honduras followed the same pattern," writes Albert L. Huebner. "So did Nicaragua until 1979, when the Somoza dictatorship was overthrown. Under that plundering regime, beef production increased threefold after 1960, but beef exports increased nearly six-fold. The Somoza family owned one-fourth of the country's farmland, as well as six beef-importing companies in Miami." (See "World Hunger Myths: Taking Food From the Poor's Mouths," Albert L. Huebner, *The Nation*, June 22, 1985.) In light of such looting, it should become clearer, even to the dimmest deep ecologist, why nationalist regimes that cease to serve as simple conduits for massive U.S. corporate exploitation come under such powerful attack — Guatemala in 1954, Chile in 1973, and now Nicaragua, to name just a few. Ironically, in contrast to Dave Foreman's paranoid desire to protect "the resources we have" in the U.S. from famished Latin Americans, the State Department philosophy since the 1950s has been to rely on various police states and to hold back "nationalistic regimes" that might be more responsive to "increasing popular demand for immediate improvement in the low living standards of the masses," in order to "protect our resources" — in their countries! Hence the current genocidal war against Central America. (See "The Scandals of 1986," by Noam Chomsky, in the Spring/Summer 1987 *Our Generation*. Also his *Turning the Tide: U.S. Intervention in Central America and the Struggle for Peace*, South End Press, 1985, which should be read by every deep ecologist.)

Despite many informative articles, and much activity in behalf of rainforests, the connection between human suffering and habitat destruction is rarely made in *Earth First!* For information on rainforests write to the Rainforest Action Network, 301 Broadway, Suite A, San Francisco, CA 94133. *The World Rainforest Report* formerly appeared as a supplement in *Earth First!*, but had a somewhat different perspective, as far as I could tell, on the population question. One such supplement contained an article on deforestation in the Philippines stressing that while population pressure "has been the common scapegoat for many ills in developing countries," and while such pressure "will have a direct impact on forest destruction in the Philippines," it is poverty that underlies the problem. The way to promote smaller families, the author argued, is "to provide livelihoods allowing for a life of dignity." Despite serious population increase, "existing sources would have sufficed" in many situations "had there been equitable distribution." He gave as an example the island of Palawan, where the upland forests are being destroyed by poor farmers while the lowlands, held by absentee landlords, sit idle.

[14] This is not the image of world hunger held by most North Americans. Rather, the U.S. is seen as the "breadbasket of the world," feeding the poor nations and keeping them from even more severe misery than they are currently undergoing. "The truth," writes Huebner in the article cited above, "is quite different." In 1978, for example, "a representative year between periods of famine, most U.S. agricultural exports went to well-fed nations, not to those where malnutrition is pervasive. And for all the importance placed on breadbaskets, only one fifth of the grain in international trade goes to less-developed countries." If we look at protein deficiency, which, according to world hunger analyst George Borgström, "must be regarded as the chief nutritional deficiency of the world," protein is flowing from the poor to the rich nations. "Rather than the rich feeding the poor," write Huebner, "the poor feed the rich."

The U.S., for example, imports more meat than it exports; in 1977, it exported about $600 billion, but imported twice that amount. U.S. imports of fish have risen as well, doubling since the 1950s. During 1971, when a previous famine wracked Africa, 56 million pounds of fish were exported from the hardest-hit regions. In Malaysia, despite a "substantial increase in the total catch" between 1967 and 1975, "per capita fish consumption dropped by 30 percent. In Thailand and the Philippines, seafood exports have also increased rapidly while local consumption has declined."

"Because the poor are feeding the rich," Huebner concludes, "famine in many parts of the world will increase." And increasing exports, which is the statist strategy, will only exacerbate the problem. Africa offers "a striking illustration," according to Huebner. "Media accounts portray the continent's food problem as a blend of drought, disease, overpopulation, political instability, and inefficient peasant farming. The prevailing sense is that Africa is a basket case which will survive only through massive, open-ended aid. In fact, it is a rich and steady source of crops consumed daily in the advanced nations — meat, vegetables, tea, coffee, cocoa, sugar — and even of fresh flowers for the dinner table. Increased exports will profit international agribusiness, which dominates Third World agricultural production, and will maintain the large landholders there, but it won't feed hungry Africans."

The strategy of self-sufficiency, while a "more promising" one, he explains, is also flawed: "Self-sufficiency in less-developed countries can't happen until it is practiced by the developed nations, and they relinquish their control of the world food system. . . . The question, What can poor countries do to become self-sufficient? requires a small, but critical change to What can rich countries do to become self-sufficient?"

[15] Greg Kaza in "The Poisoning of America," Detroit *Metro Times*, January 6-12, 1988.

[16] In some countries the lack of land, unemployment, and plummeting wages have reversed this tendency, and population growth may be starting to bottom out. According to Harrison, Bali, Thailand, Indonesia, and Egypt have seen significant drops in their growth rates due to a combination of landlessness, unemployment, and vigorous family-planning programs. Lappé and Collins argue, "In countries where the decline in birth rate has been significant, the causal factors do not appear to be direct birth control programs so much as a shift in resources toward the poorest groups." In countries such as Sri Lanka, Singapore, Hong Kong, Taiwan, Egypt, Argentina, Uruguay, Costa Rica, and Cuba, "most have, or once had, some national policies favoring the low-income groups, whereas in countries such as Brazil, Venezuela, the Philippines and Mexico, the well-being of low-income groups is diminishing, and birth rates are not declining significantly."

Woman's Freedom: Key to the Population Question

A Review of *Reproductive Rights and Wrongs: The Global Politics of Population Control and Contraceptive Choice*, by Betsy Hartmann, Harper & Row, New York, 1987.

This impassioned inquiry is both important and timely. It is important because it synthesizes valuable research to reveal the interlocking connections between world population growth and the related questions of hunger, ecological devastation, political economy, human health, and human rights. It is timely because it adds a much-needed dimension to the critique of the Malthusian orthodoxy that overpopulation is the underlying cause of hunger and that population control is the solution. It focuses on the social relations that underlie both the population explosion and the global strategies to confront it, and ties together the discussions of world ecological crisis, the contemporary battle over reproductive rights (including abortion), the question of population control, and human rights in the Third World. Much of this is addressed in Lappé and Collins's book *Food First*, but by exploring the areas of population control, women's reproductive rights, and all human rights, Hartmann adds much to the entire discussion.

The book reflects what Hartmann describes as "an ongoing process" of thinking about the population question, and is based on several years of research as well as direct experience living in a rural village in Bangladesh during the mid-1970s. It is a valuable contribution to what should be an ongoing process of inquiry for us all. Her message is that the way out of the current impasse and drift toward greater catastrophe, the way toward stable population levels *and* ecological and human well-being, is the same. Furthermore, it is distinctly liberatory, centering as it does on the rights of women not only to their own reproductive destiny, but to participate fully in society. Thus it moves dramatically away from an authoritarian, bureaucratic-technological domain toward a participatory, liberatory vision of human empowerment and health.

That the liberation of women is the key to the crisis is an important and compelling insight, and suggests very strongly the connection between empire, the destruction of the natural world, the human/nature split, and the original emergence of institutions of domination over women. Such a discussion affirms two anarchist and eco-feminist perspectives. Firstly, the fundamental causes of our present crisis in nature and culture lie in the origins and consolidation of the institutions of human (particularly male) domination. Secondly the way out of the crisis lies in the practical opening toward freedom of self-expression and selfhood for women that is the key to the destruction of hierarchy, the re-empowerment of human communities, access to and proper relations with the land, and human health.

This very clear picture elaborates a tragically obscured dimension: *how* exactly, "The needs of the planet are the needs of the person," and "The rights of the person are the rights of the planet," to use Theodore Roszak's excellent formulation. The salvation of the marvelous green planet, our Mother Earth, depends on the liberation of women — and children, and men — from social domination, exploitation and hierarchy. They must go together. Neither a radical political vision nor a profound ecological vision can exist without this fundamental dimension.

The Two Sides of Birth Control

Hartmann's book is refreshing in that, instead of going into a long description of population growth itself, she provides a history of fertility control. Many traditions, such as abstinence and withdrawal, and techniques, such as abortion and barrier methods of contraception (like a cervical sponge or diaphragm), are thousands of years old. Some 400 species of flowering plants grown in 111 countries have been used traditionally for fertility control. Condoms, too, are quite old, and by the 1800s the process of vulcanization made possible much-improved condoms and diaphragms.

Fertility control hardly starts with Malthus, who in fact had opposed contraception as immoral, preferring to let the poor starve as a "natural" method of keeping numbers down. For him, only misery, poverty, famine, disease, and war would keep population from expanding beyond the carrying capacity of the land.

Many working-class radicals accepted the logic that excessive numbers were what kept the poor in their misery. During the nineteenth century there were courageous attempts to disseminate birth-control information both to promote lower population and to make it possible for women to control their own reproductivity and escape male domination. Birth control was the province of feminism, radical socialism, and anarchism. Emma Goldman, for example, was arrested and jailed for distributing a pamphlet, *Why and How the Poor Should Not Have Many Children,* which described condoms, cervical caps, and diaphragms. Birth-control clinics were opened by socialists in Europe, and in Germany female members forced the Social Democratic Party to reverse its opposition to birth control. In the United States, a young social activist, Margaret Sanger, founded *The Woman Rebel,* a paper with a socialist-feminist and pro-reproductive-choice perspective, which was shut down by the post office. Sanger had to flee to Europe after being indicted on two counts of obscenity. Later the charges were dropped, but she was arrested for opening a birth-control clinic in Brooklyn.

The key to the breakdown in the alliance between radicals and the birth-control movement toward the end of the second decade of the twentieth century is suggested by Hartmann's comment that the birth-control movement had "carried within it the seeds of birth control as a liberating force as well as a means of coercive population control." Two other sources of the birth-control movement had also emerged, the eugenics movement, which argued for the "improvement of breeds" through genetic manipulation, and the desire by the professional medical establishment to bring birth control and reproductive decisions under its own supervision. As repression set in and the radical movement waned in the late teens and early 1920s, Sanger herself moved to the right, seeking respectability and an alliance with elitist medical professionals. (Those readers familiar with Ivan Illich's thoughtful descriptions of the professional monopolization and institutionalization of health and their subsequent destruction of human community, subsistence values, and the possibility for more liberatory modes of health, will recognize this process in the birth-control movement's evolution. See *Medical Nemesis* and *Toward a History of Needs.*)

With the hierarchicization of birth control, and the retreat by anticapitalist radicals from feminist issues, the movement became increasingly reactionary, with racist, nationalist, and fascist elements creeping in. By 1919 Sanger was writing that the "degenerate" masses might destroy "our way of life," and arguing, "More children from the fit and less from the unfit — that is the chief issue of birth control." By 1932 she was calling for sterilization and segregation by sex of the "dysgenic population," a program which would soon be carried out with a vengeance by the Nazis, who in 1933 passed their first sterilization laws for people deemed "unfit." This slippery slope ended in mass extermination practices and mass starvation of psychiatric inmates and others. Although Nazi brutality discredited eugenist ideology in the U.S., Hartmann observes, "that ideology never completely disappeared."

With the New Deal and the reorganization of capital in the 1930s and 1940s, birth control was once more linked ideologically with social reform. This period was marked by the emergence of the real (as opposed to formal) domination of capital and the integration of proletarian movements and their program into the institutions of a modernized capitalist state. With World War II, the consolidation of what Lewis Mumford has described as the nuclear-cybernetic megamachine was complete; the Nazi vision of the superstate had won the war in the newly emerged garrison states that had defeated the Axis powers. In the area of birth control, the same ambivalent character remained. Planned Parenthood made contraceptive techniques available for millions of women. As a result, capital was able to integrate women into industry and bring about further transformation of the proletariat for its own purposes of rationalization.

Population Control and the Cold War

Perhaps the most interesting section of this history is the origin of modern birth and population control as a component of the Cold War. The desire of the United States to "contain communism" and control the resources and political developments of the so-called "Grand Area" (essentially everywhere outside the Eastern Bloc), led to a perspective of population control to thwart nationalist revolt in the Third World. The Chinese and Vietnamese revolutions frightened U.S. ruling circles, as did Indian and Indonesian independence and nonalignment. The concern, of course, was the "security" of raw materials to feed the Garrison State. Governments in Iran, Guatemala, Indonesia, and Brazil, among others, had to be overthrown to protect the "Grand Area" from internal aggression (that is, from their own populations), and Indochina was militarily attacked for several decades to stem the tide of nationalist revolt and war against the landlords and corporate puppets, until the region was effectively shattered socially and ecologically.

Nationalist independence and realignment were seen by foreign-policy circles as direct results of population pressure as far back as the early 1950s, and such pressure was therefore a priority for the U.S. policy establishment. The 1957 Ad Hoc Committee report "depicted population growth as a major threat to political stability both at home and abroad," writes Hartmann. By 1967, advertisements from the population-control lobby (heavily financed and promoted by Dixie Cup magnate Hugh Moore) asserted, "The ever-mounting tidal wave of humanity now challenges us to control it or be submerged along with all our civilized values," and, "A world with mass starvation in underdeveloped countries will be a world of chaos, riots and war. And a perfect breeding ground for Communism. . . . We cannot afford a half dozen Vietnams or even one more. . . . Our own national interest demands that we go all out to help the underdeveloped countries control their population."

Such control was always seen as a process of collaboration with local elites through military aid and the establishment of state-dominated institutions for population control. In fact, the U.S. Agency for International Development (AID) is presently the largest single funder of population activities in the Third World. Local revolts, as in Central America, were and are consistently blamed on population pressure rather than on class war and domination. This explains vividly the contemporary configuration of the population establishment and its technocratic vision of population control linked to industrial development, urbanization, and the world commodity market, exemplified by technocrats like Robert McNamara, former U.S. Secretary of Defense and head of the World Bank. It also aptly reveals how the Reaganite position against abortion rights in the Third World, based on the absurd "cornucopia thesis" of consultants like Herbert Kahn (that denies *any* necessary limitations to population growth), is only an aberration in an overall global strategy, a sop to Reagan's right-wing, fundamentalist supporters inside the U.S. The anti-population-control statement of the U.S. at the August 1984 Mexico City Conference on Population, in fact, was designed for domestic consumption, and "served to legitimize the position of the population establishment by casting them in the role of the defenders of reproductive rights," and masking their real role as institutions of authoritarian-statist control.

Authoritarian and Technocratic

The contemporary population-control establishment is, indeed, a component of the same forces of plunder and oppression that have brought the world to the brink of an ecological and social abyss. Its focus is authoritarian and technocratic. It follows a "machine model" perspective of human reproductive decision-making and has a high-tech preference for sterilization, IUD's, the pill, and other risky forms of fertility control, over traditional methods and barrier techniques. It avoids any discussion of the social context within which reproductive decisions are made (or not made), defends the status quo of stratified, class societies and the capitalist market, and actually discourages an overall approach to women's and children's primary health as a central factor in population stabilization. Population bureaucrats deal with people in a purely instrumental fashion as statistics, and "incentive" programs are followed to sterilize as many people as possible, no matter what.

The ideology of population control is summed up by Hartmann as based on three tenets:

"1. Rapid population growth is a primary cause of the Third World's development problems, notably hunger, environmental destruction, economic stagnation, and political instability." Notice that it is *development* itself (which means capital accumulation), and not environmental and human well-being, which is the central concern. People are "units."

"2. People must be persuaded — or forced, if necessary — to have fewer children without fundamentally improving the impoverished conditions in which they live." Such improvement, of course, would demand agrarian and social revolution, which would undermine both the local elites and ultimately, perhaps, the entire development model of industrial-capitalist civilization.

"3. Given the right combination of finance, personnel, technology, and Western management techniques, birth-control services can be 'delivered' to Third World women in a top-down fashion and in the absence of basic health-care systems. In both the development and promotion of contraceptives, efficacy in preventing pregnancy should take precedence over health and safety concerns." One can see the entire operationalism of mass technology and the disabling professions at work in this assumption.

Underlying the entire population control ideology is Malthusian orthodoxy, which argues that the earth has reached the limits of its carrying capacity due to excessive human numbers using resources excessively. The image of a dark-skinned woman far along in her pregnancy is supposed to bring to mind the source of the world's miseries. Hartmann does a good job of putting this orthodoxy into a proper perspective. Those who see the problem "as an inevitable race between man and nature" have a point, she writes. "No one wants a world of standing room only, where every bit of land, drop of water, and unit of energy is pressed into producing sustenance for an endlessly expanding human mass. Other species have a right to inhabit the earth, and our own quality of life is enhanced by respect for the natural environment. However, while limiting human numbers makes sense in the long run, it does not follow that in the short run overpopulation is the main cause of environmental depletion."

Yet it is not so much the population growth that puts pressure on the earth as it is "the consumption explosion in the industrialized world," she argues. "Moreover . . . many of the main ecological crimes being perpetrated on the earth" are caused by "unregulated and inappropriate patterns of technological development" rather than the population growth of peasants. Hartmann looks at the arguments for environmental destruction as an outcome of population pressure and finds them seriously flawed.

Malthusian Fatalism

One instance is the serious problem of deforestation, which according to the official view of the Indian government, for example, was caused primarily by population pressure. Yet when the Center for Science and the Environment in New Delhi investigated deforestation there, where millions of hectares of forest are disappearing annually, it found that private companies had "illegally felled huge sections of India's forests, at the same time as they were declared off limits to the local communities who have long depended on them for a livelihood. Meanwhile, 'official' forestry projects, aided by international agencies such as the World Bank, are encouraging the export of India's hardwoods and the destruction of mixed, ecologically sound forests in favor of monoculture plantations of pine, eucalyptus, and teak." The same process is going on throughout the Third World, as in Brazil, where corporations like Goodyear, Volkswagen, Nestlé and Mitsubishi have stripped millions of acres of rainforest for lumber and cattle ranching. While dictator of the Philippines, Ferdinand Marcos "gave illegal logging concessions worth over a billion dollars to relatives and political cronies, depleting the country's forest reserves from 34.6 million acres in 1965, when Marcos took power, to only 5.4 million acres [in 1987]."

Desertification, like deforestation, is largely a result of inequities on and exploitation of the land. A world land census in 1960 revealed that 2.5 percent of landowners controlled 75 percent of arable land in the world, and the top 0.23 percent controlled over half. And where starvation ravaged the poor, those regions, as in the famished Sahel of Africa, actually increased agricultural exports. In Burkina Faso (formerly Upper Volta) in West Africa, Hartmann reports that cotton production increased twenty times since 1961, while staple crops like millet and sorghum remained at 1960 levels. The same situation is occurring in El Salvador, where 77 percent of the land faces accelerated erosion; most of the poor are marginalized on higher slopes, causing ecological damage, and the good lands are monopolized by the death-squad oligarchy to raise exports like cotton, coffee, sugar, and cattle. "In such a situation," Hartmann writes, "more people do mean more ecological destruction, since they are crowded into a limited land space. In this sense, rapid population growth is a factor in desertification, but to call it the primary cause is to simplify a much more complex process. El Salvador's peasants are putting pressure on marginal lands because they themselves have been made marginal by an agricultural system controlled by the rich."

Hartmann comes to the same conclusions as Lappé and Collins: "Despite the popular Western image of the Third World as a bottomless begging bowl," she observes, "it today gives more to the industrialized world than it takes. Inflows of official 'aid' and private loans and investments are exceeded by outflows in the form of repatriated profits, interest payments, and private capital sent abroad by Third World elites." According to one banking study, more than a third of the region's increase in borrowing between 1978 and 1983 was "spirited away overseas" by rich Latin Americans.

When the Malthusians do ask why people are going hungry, why they lack livelihoods, why they are driven from their land, they do not consider the questions of land ownership, the history of colonialism, and where social power lies. So when the poor demand their rights, the Malthusians see "political instability" growing from population pressure. "Their ideological fervor masks a profound fatalism: the poor are born to their lot, and the only way out for them is to stop being born." "Population control is substituted for social justice, and the problem is actually aggravated by the Malthusian 'cure.'" Family planning and health are subordinated to coercive and repressive population control, and millions of women are negatively affected.

Both the failures and the "successes" of authoritarian population control are explored at length by Hartmann. In Bangladesh, for example, "Spending on population control now absorbs over one third of the country's annual health budget, and its share is growing." Health care for mothers and children is being slashed to pay for population programs. Population-control efforts are being accelerated as the quality of life deteriorates, through landlessness, plummeting wages, decreasing food consumption. More than 60 percent of the population now has an inadequate diet. Amazingly, "Despite the millions of dollars flowing into the country for population control, women's need for contraception is still not being met. . . . Whereas before village women were neglected by Bangladesh's family planning program, now they are the targets of an aggressive sterilization drive that uses incentives and intimidation to produce results. Meanwhile, access to safe and reversible methods of fertility control is still very limited." Sterilizations, for which a person might be paid a small sum and given some new clothes, "increase dramatically during the lean autumn months before the rice harvest, when many landless peasants are unemployed and destitute." The sterilization methods themselves are brutal and impersonal, and frequently lead to complications, illness and even death, since follow-up medical aid is unavailable.

Population Control as Genocide

The genocidal character of population control is dizzying. Sterilization has been focused on India's tribal minorities, though they are numerically small. In South Africa, population control is for blacks, while whites are rewarded for having children. The only free medical service for blacks is birth control. There, the argument is used widely that black "overpopulation" is putting pressure on the ecology of the region. In Puerto Rico, a U.S. colony ecologically devastated by U.S. corporate exploitation (and where mainland U.S. environmental laws do not apply), one third of the women were sterilized by 1968. Inside the U.S., Native American women have been the target of forced sterilization. China, which has recently been going through economic transformations along a Western development model, has implemented draconian antipopulation measures, with forced abortions and sterilizations to impose a one-child-family policy. As new incentive programs along private capitalist lines have been implemented, Malthus has slipped in with them. Nevertheless, interestingly, China's greatest strides in stabilizing population came before the one-child policy was instituted, according to Hartmann, and there has even been a slight population trend upward since the new policy, along with the privatization of lands, was implemented.

It should come as no surprise that this "profoundly technocratic exercise" should aggravate the problem and backfire. The notion that top-down techniques and "rational" education of the poor, administered by authoritarian, privileged elites over the peasants who are their subjects, without reference to the social context of land ownership, social power, and health, is a scientistic and mechanistic fantasy. But it is the strategy followed by most Third World states and Western population and family-planning agencies. Kenya is considered one of the worst failures of such policy, yet it was the first African nation south of the Sahara to implement an official population-control program, in 1967. Because it ignored social and economic conditions, and focused on population control rather than family planning and health, it was resisted by the people, and now Kenya has one of the highest birth rates in the world. None of the sources of high fertility — high infant mortality, landlessness, lack of power, patriarchal domination — was addressed. One of the largest causes of high dropout rates in family planning was contraceptive side effects, yet riskier high-tech methods were favored, and local custom and health devalued, so women did not respond.

The "machine model of family planning," based on efficiency models, incentives, and "target orientation," ends in outright coercion. In Indonesia, which is ruled by a right-wing dictatorship, "women are dragooned toward contraception as, once, they were doomed to uncontrolled fertility."

Choice is actually limited to the worst techniques, and traditional methods and low-tech methods demanding women's empowerment and participation as well as a focus on their health, are actively discriminated against. Even the military authorities have been directly involved, forcing IUD's on villagers at gunpoint. "The top-down approach toward birth-control means it is not popularly perceived as a tool of reproductive choice," writes Hartmann almost euphemistically, "but as a means of social control." One can see this process backfiring as it did in Kenya and may be starting to do in China. Yet, startlingly, "Indonesia has become *the* family planning showcase of the Third World."

Ironically, the women of the world *want* birth-control. Hartmann discusses several studies, including a survey done in 27 Third World countries, that found that "almost half the married women questioned wanted no more children, and that younger women especially tended to desire a smaller family size." Women actually lack access to birth control and information. The 30 to 50 million induced abortions a year — one half of them illegal — also suggest that women want birth control. (In Latin America, up to one half of all maternal deaths are due to illegal abortions.)

An Expansion of Rights

Thus the Malthusians have the problem backward, she argues. "The solution to the population problem lies not in the diminution of rights, but in their *expansion*. This is because the population problem is not really about a surplus of human numbers, but a lack of basic human rights." One of the main reasons for high birth rates is a total lack of security, which means that people gamble on having large families, particularly sons, with their old age, illness, and economic dislocation in mind. High infant-mortality rates are also a cause of high fertility. One would think, as do many contemporary Malthusians, "that reductions of infant mortality would actually *increase* the rate of population growth, since there would be more surviving children to grow up into fertile adults." (One AID bureaucrat even argued that primary-health-care programs should be discouraged, since they might aggravate the population problem by lowering death rates.) "Experience has shown," Hartmann asserts, "that once mortality rates fall to around 15 per 1000 people per year, the average for the Third World today, each further decline in the mortality rate is generally accompanied by an even greater decline in the birth rate, as people adjust their fertility to improved survival possibilities." High birth rates flow directly from high infant-mortality rates, and the latter are "primarily caused by poor nutrition, both of the mother and the child." Nutrition is crucial, even more important than primary health care itself, since it underlies the whole chain of causes of infant mortality, from unhealthy mothers to low birth weight to poor breast milk. Paradoxically, what one United Nations official has called a "survival revolution," halving the infant-and-child mortality rate and preventing the deaths of six or seven million infants each year by the end of the century, could also prevent between 12 and 20 million births annually. Hartmann remarks, "To date no country has achieved a low birth rate as long as it has had a high infant mortality rate."

In countries like Sri Lanka, Cuba, and the Indian state of Kerala, where the birth rates have been dramatically lowered, it is not so much that industrial development, measured in terms of increased energy consumption and personal income per capita, has improved the standard of living, but that basic nutrition and access to primary health care and reproductive choice have been emphasized. Ironically, if the Malthusians have their way and health and nutrition in the Third World are allowed to decline even further as the Malthusian "checks" take their toll, the population explosion will only be exacerbated. By ideologizing the population question to the detriment of social critique, they work to promote the very scenario they claim to fear most.

The question, of course, goes beyond population control and family planning. Women's reproductive choice depends on their role in society as a whole, and their lack of choice is directly linked to their lack of autonomy and personhood as well as to their economic domination. Women are invisible in official labor statistics, but research shows that "women produce almost half the food crops grown in the world. In Africa women contribute two-thirds of all hours spent in traditional agriculture and three-fifths of the time spent in marketing. In Asia, they constitute over half the agricultural labor force; in Latin America at least 40 percent." Modernization, of course, has worsened women's lot. Commercial farming has favored men at every level, and industrialization only doubles women's workload. Today 80 to 90 percent of low-skilled assembly jobs in the Third World are held by women.

Women's freedom and well-being are at the center of the resolution to the population problem, and that can only be faced within the larger social context. Even health and family-planning programs will not suffice if they are implemented from above and administered as a technological procedure. If primary health care is to be used effectively, it must take place within "fundamental power struggles," which means real participation in social decision-making, real health concerns, access to land, and the overthrow of patriarchal domination. "There is no intrinsic reason why women's health and safety have to be sacrificed to contraceptive efficacy or why freedom of choice has to be subordinated to population control," writes Hartmann. "If there is to be a second contraceptive revolution, let it start with a revolution in values."

Personal, Political, Planetary

What would be the focus of such values? Woman must be at the center of concern — her autonomy and her well-being and the well-being of her children, within the larger social context of access to land and participation in society. If the origins of hierarchy and domination as well as humanity's anguished cleft with the natural world are to be found in woman's primordial enslavement and the institutionalization of patriarchy, then the necessity of her liberation is an elegant testimonial to the working-out of a historical dialectic, a return to origins, a completion of a cycle. This can only come about by abolishing the structures of domination which are globally undermining women's freedom and health, and leading the planet to catastrophe. The political, the personal, and the planetary all find expression in this process of liberation.

Some criticisms can be made of Hartmann's book. She appears at times to be impressed with industrial growth as a solution to the problem of domination and hunger. She is also too willing to make use of arguments against Malthusianism that depend on industrial and technological models of development and beg the question of carrying capacity. One need not repeat the arguments of some historians that population growth is the cause of improvements in conditions; it only legitimates industrialism while evading the central question of massive population growth as a result of the disruption of traditional societies and natural economies. The discussion of Africa is an example, in which Hartmann argues that Africa was to some degree *depopulated* by the slave trade, and while it was 20 percent of the world's population in the eighteenth century, by the year 2000 it will be less than 13 percent. These figures are meaningless. The slave trade had little or no effect at all on numbers in Africa, as any population atlas will attest, except to disrupt the local societies enough to cause further population growth. Africa is not in need of more hands to promote development. And Africa needs, for its long-term health and biotic diversity, to leave most of its uncultivated lands as they are. If the population question is an ongoing process of inquiry, Hartmann should go on to pursue a critique of industrialism, technological development, the disempowerment and commoditization of human communities, and the creation of mass society. A revolution in values demands a critique of industrial civilization and an attempt to live in harmony with the natural integrity of the planet, not mass industrial complexes to build tractors or produce chemical fertilizers.

This is not the focus of Hartmann's book, which is, rather, the question of women's reproductive rights as a central factor in their human rights, as integral to the entire project of social transformation and human freedom. Her devastating critique of authoritarian technocratic population control suggests a deeper critique of modern technological civilization, rationalization, and modernization, even if it is beyond the scope of the book to explore those themes further. Perhaps it is beyond any single book to provide such a critique. Readers can do that on their own by sifting through a whole body of literature and personal experience. Nevertheless, Hartmann has made an extremely valuable contribution to the critique of Malthusian ideology and has added important insights by linking the resolution of the population problem and the ecological crisis to the project of human liberation — for that she deserves our praise and gratitude.

Other books from
TIMES CHANGE PRESS

THE TRAFFIC IN WOMEN and Other Essays on Feminism — Emma Goldman; with a biography by Alix Kates Shulman. Emma Goldman was a dynamic anarchist whose feminism differed markedly from that of her suffrage-oriented contemporaries. The split between liberal and radical approaches to women's liberation is still not resolved, so her essays have an uncanny relevancy to problems now being dealt with. 7th printing. *Illustrated; 64 pp; $3.00*

GENERATIONS OF DENIAL: 75 Short Biographies of Women in History — Kathryn Taylor. These women were whole people under the worst of circumstances, worse still for those who, in addition to being female, were gay. These biographies are a pioneering collection with which to supplement history books and women's pride. 4th printing. *Illustrated; 64 pp; $3.00*

FREE SPACE: A Perspective on the Small Group in Women's Liberation — Pamela Allen. *Free Space* is a good handbook for people wondering how to begin or restructure a consciousness-raising group. Developed by feminists, the small group is now being used by many people as a way of relating to different needs. 3d printing of 2d edition, revised. *Illustrated; 64 pp; $2.95*

SOME PICTURES FROM MY LIFE: A Diary — Marcia Salo Rizzi. Marcia has selected entries from her diary and combined them with her emotionally powerful ink-brush drawings — one woman's experience reflecting pictures from the lives of all women. *Illustrated; 64 pp; $2.95*

**FOR MEN AGAINST SEXISM: A Book of Readings —
Edited by Jon Snodgrass.** Men deeply influenced by feminism analyze and share personal experiences of male sexuality and socialization, recent actions to combat sexism, and the special oppressions of Third World, working-class, and gay men. These men's goal: to transform themselves and revolutionize patriarchal society. 4th printing. *240 pp; $7.95*

FATHERJOURNAL: Five Years of Awakening to Fatherhood — David Steinberg. This is a sensitive, unglorified account of a father who decides not to become "the second, somewhat foreign parent." Instead, he seeks intimate, nurturing contact with his child, and reveals for us the resulting emotional and sex-role conflicts, as well as the new levels of love and awareness that fatherhood opens to him. 3d printing. *Illustrated; 96 pp; $4.95*

THE EARLY HOMOSEXUAL RIGHTS MOVEMENT (1864-1935) — John Lauritsen and David Thorstad. The gay movement, like the women's movement, has an early history which, beginning in 1864, advanced the cause of gay rights until the 1930s, when Stalinist and Nazi repression obliterated virtually all traces of it. The authors uncover this history, highlighting interesting people and events. 3d printing. *Illustrated; 96 pp. Cloth, $10.95*